D1474986

LEARNING

FROM

EXPERIENCE

LEARNING

FROM

EXPERIENCE

A GUIDEBOOK FOR CLINICIANS

MARILYN CHARLES

With a Foreword by Nancy McWilliams

 THE ANALYTIC PRESS

2004   Hillsdale, NJ   London

Published by
The Analytic Press, Inc., Publishers
Editorial Offices:
101 West Street
Hillsdale, NJ 07642

www.analyticpress.com

Designed and typeset by Compudesign, Charlottesville, VA.

Library of Congress Cataloging-in-Publication Data

Charles, Marilyn.
    Learning from experience : a guidebook for clinicians /
Marilyn Charles.
        p. ; cm.
    Includes bibliographical references and index.
    ISBN 0-88163-410-7
        1. Psychoanalysis.   2. Psychoanalysis—Vocational guidance.
    3. Psychotherapist and patient.   I. Title.

[DNLM: 1. Psychoanalytic Therapy. 2. Psychotherapeutic Processes.
WM 460.6 C476L 2004]

RC504.C48 2004
150.19'5—dc22

                                                                    2004046150

Printed in the United States of America

10 9 8 7 6 5 4 3 2

Contents

Foreword

IN *LEARNING FROM EXPERIENCE,* Marilyn Charles has written a meditation on emotional growth, on coming to know and be one's full self, that embodies as well as describes its subject. There are many good texts on how to do psychoanalytic therapy and how to understand what happens in psychoanalytic therapy. But there are very few that bring the reader so intimately inside the experience of both therapist and patient, that capture the music as well as the words of the therapeutic project. Charles maintains an unprecedented level of empathy with her readers. Inviting the beginning therapist to feel the nuances of an art that stubbornly resists reduction, she demystifies the mysterious without profaning the mystery. She interprets not only theory but also the process and value of theory-making. With unusual grace and unwavering respect for both parties to the therapeutic collaboration, Charles brings both the torments and the joys of clinical experience to life. Rich examples elucidate the wisdom of Bion, Klein, Winnicott, Lacan, and other prophetic voices in psychoanalysis. And she keeps her focus on the task at hand: nourishing the capacity of the developing therapist to engage in the kind of intimacy that fosters genuineness and growth in another person and also in the self.

I have been particularly struck by the relevance of Charles's chapter organization to the questions most commonly asked these days by therapists in training. The conventional, ego-psychology-generated parsing of psychoanalytic clinical knowledge into categories such as the working alliance, resistance, transference, countertransference, working through, and termination has become rather distant from the bedrock questions about being, feeling, and knowing that assail the newer therapist. Contemporary patients seldom look like the "neurotics" of an earlier era. They are more likely to come to treatment with problems in feeling alive, regulating affect, and staying honest, miseries that Westen has aptly called "cancers of the soul." They radiate desperation. Topics such as the role of theory, the container and contained, the schizoid and depressive positions, transitional space, truth and lies, and expanding a space for play speak far more pointedly to the urgent needs of current practitioners than an earlier psychoanalytic language which assumed a self that could observe its problematic components.

Contemporary students of psychoanalytic therapy are confronted with a bewildering barrage of theoretical models and therapeutic metaphors. If they are exposed to psychoanalytic thinking in graduate school or medical training—and increasingly, they are not, given the ascendancy of cognitive-behavioral paradigms in psychology and biological models in psychiatry—the emphasis is likely to be on the short-term, symptom-targeted, empirically researched psychodynamic approaches. If they become attracted (usually as a result of their personal therapy, their independent reading, or their experience with psychoanalytic supervisors) to a psychodynamic sensibility, they may be confronted with the work of thinkers as diverse as Heinz Hartmann and Melanie Klein, Margaret Mahler and Harold Searles, Otto Kernberg and Heinz Kohut, Donald Winnicott and Jacques Lacan, James Masterson and Wilfred Bion, Jessica Benjamin and Robert Wallerstein, Salman Akhtar and Karen Maroda, Joseph Weiss and Thomas Ogden. Unlike beginning therapists a generation ago, who could master the Freud canon and then diversify into ego psychology or the British object relations tradition or the American interpersonal movement or the nascent developments in self psychology and intersubjectivity, newcomers to the field today first have to stake out their claim to psychoanalytic as opposed to other paradigms and then find themselves recruited by representatives of wildly disparate sensibilities. It is a wonder they find their way.

Charles's contribution should make it easer for them. It is not a simple matter to render theorists like Klein and Bion into user-friendly authorities. Much more than Freud did, they wrote about preverbal, right-brained processes that do not lend themselves readily to explication via the written word. Their writing is dense, passionate, revelatory, poetic—a startling contrast to the tone of mainstream academic/medical discourse. Because such writers mine the territory of the intuitive and the impressionistic, they speak eloquently to the affective experience of clinicians, but their accessibility is limited by the ineffable nature of their subject. When beginning therapists start to see how flimsy is the life raft of their intellectual preparation to survive the sea of suffering they are plunged into by their patients' pain, they need the wisdom of thinkers like the ones Charles has assimilated, and they need it translated into clinical vignettes with which they can identify, summarized in a voice that feels calming, steadying, still afloat. In my view, this is the primary interpretive achievement of this book.

Its emotional achievements include Charles's unfailing faith in the clinical process and respect for her readers' capacities to engage in it. She maintains the focus on the beginner without ever talking down to her audience. She understands the practicing clinician's need for integration rather than critical dissection of theory. She shares the myths and narratives that have illuminated her own therapeutic journey without needing to diminish alternative sources of illumination that have done the same job for others. Her pleasure, related in her concluding comments, in realizing that she and Philip Bromberg were talking about the same phenomena in different languages is a familiar experience to those of us with years of clinical seasoning and will be a relief to readers who have been told that they must learn one set of metaphors at the expense of others. Charles's application of empirical findings in cognitive neuroscience and affect theory to the clinical project attests to the breadth of her synthetic capacity. Not to mention the integration of her own prior contributions, which, via this volume, are now more available to newcomers to the field.

Many psychoanalytic scholars write for each other. Charles has written for the next generation of analytic therapists and for those outside the profession who want to reach a sophisticated object-relations vantage point without wading through a swamp of abstraction and obfuscation. In a very small space, she has managed to convey the experiential essence of both psychoanalytic therapy and the innate potential for human growth that it seeks to liberate. *Learning from Experience* is a helpful book for more professionally mature psychotherapists as well, but I take an especially keen pleasure in anticipating assigning it to my students.

NANCY MCWILLIAMS, PH.D.

Acknowledgments

THE SUPERVISORY PROCESS has been a source of great pleasure for me. One challenge has been to try to translate into usable terms psychoanalytic conceptualizations that can be quite unapproachable for the novice and yet can also be extraordinarily constructive. This book had its origins in my desire to make these ideas more accessible to supervisees, who were so clearly enlivened when they began to really 'get' a concept that had previously eluded them. Their understanding was inevitably guided by their ability to connect those conceptualizations to their own experiences.

I am grateful to all of the individuals who have invited me into their journeys, either as patients or as students. The hours spent exploring the complex terrain of human experience have been immeasurably rewarding. I truly believe that we learn best and most constructively through our own experience, and hope that in sharing my experiences in this book I will encourage others to take their own experience more seriously, to use their own senses and to fine-tune their own intuitions. Theory, like any other tool, is only as useful as our skill and understanding can make it.

Special thanks go to the students who have shared with me their experiences and insights over the years. Their enthusiasm, acuity, and tenacity in finding their way through very difficult territory continually renews my faith in the power of the human spirit. I am particularly appreciative of the efforts of Devon

Charles and Benjamin Addleson, whose thoughtful and insightful readings of previous versions of the book helped me to refine my own conceptualizations in ways that greatly enriched the text.

Working with the Analytic Press has been a real pleasure. Particular thanks go to Eleanor Starke Kobrin, whose careful editing was so helpful in putting forward these ideas in their final form and to Joan Riegel, for her warmth and her skill. I owe a special debt to Paul Stepansky for his ongoing support of my work and for his very constructive editorial suggestions.

Finally, I would like to thank my family, who have tolerated all the chaos attendant to the creation of this book, and who have been my best teachers in their own unique and wonderful ways.

LEARNING

FROM

EXPERIENCE

1

Introduction

MY GOAL IN THIS VOLUME is to talk about the difficult process in which we are all engaged: that of discovering ourselves as human beings. Because of the context, we can talk in terms of becoming therapists, but we need to keep in mind that we have just moved up a register—the basic process is one of becoming ourselves.

These goals are quite similar. In my mind, they overlap because I see the quintessential task of the clinician as one of coming to know himself or herself sufficiently to be able to register the experience of the other in progressively more profound and also more useful ways.

This process begins with our own discomfort at finding ourselves sitting in the chair that has somehow become designated as that of "the authority": the person ostensibly in charge of something we haven't even begun to comprehend.

And so begins the struggle to make ourselves more comfortable by anchoring ourselves in whatever pieces of reality seem likely grounding spots, while knowing, at some level, that each of these anchors contains within it a lie. The issue of *truth* versus *lie* is an important one. I explore it in more detail in a later chapter, after looking at some basic concepts that are useful in grounding ourselves in this work. Before we begin looking at any specific concepts, however, we should address the idea of theory itself. Theories provide a means for structuring and organizing our experiences: a way of making sense of it all.

2

The Role of Theory

THEORY OFFERS US A MODEL of reality. The model provides an initial grounding, a way of locating ourselves within the context of the therapeutic environment. It helps us to organize our perceptions and provides metaphors that enable us to communicate our perceptions in useful ways. Our theories also serve to assuage our horror (and our terror) when we're faced with impossible moments in our work. They help us to develop ideas as to how we might ground ourselves in a universe gone topsy-turvy and provide a structure that better enables us to allow it to *be* topsy-turvy sufficiently to have any idea as to what we're grounding ourselves in!

In these difficult moments, our theories can provide us with an anchor, some scaffolding within which to catch ourselves when we are threatened with falling into an abyss. Theory offers a means for continuing to think when feeling has reached such peak intensity that constructive thought may be hard to come by.

Theory is, to some extent, idiosyncratic: we choose our theories because they resonate with our experiences of being in the world. They speak to us of important truths in ways that help us to organize and utilize them constructively. For me, psychoanalytic theories—object relations theories, in particular—have been most useful in helping me make sense of the complexities of human behavior and relationships.

Whatever the particulars of our chosen theories, their common function is to provide us with metaphors. Metaphors serve a crucial role when dealing with complex phenomena. First, the metaphor helps us to keep in mind multiple elements, including the relationships between the elements and the attendant affects. Second, it provides a means for sharing these complexities, for communicating them to one another. This common language enables us to hold between us the shared elements, with all the associated affect and nuance, in a way that allows us to refer back and further elaborate them over time. In this way, we can re-find important moments and meanings that might otherwise be lost or resistant to retrieval or sharing. It is, literally, a way for us to keep complex realities "in mind."

Our metaphors can be idiosyncratic or more general. The Greek myths, for example, provide useful ways of indexing particular character traits and essential human dilemmas. Bion (1977) notes that the myth of Oedipus and the biblical stories of the Tower of Babel and the Garden of Eden each provide ways of indexing the forbidden nature of the pursuit of knowledge. There are also metaphors that we derive through our work with a given individual, based on the narratives and images that evolve in our interactions. Dreams, for example, can become pivotal reference points that we refer back to repeatedly over the course of a treatment. As we develop shared meanings, metaphors provide a relatively simple way of indexing complex relationships. I will discuss the uses of myth and metaphor in greater detail in chapter 3.

In terms of our theories, however, the ideas depicted within a given theoretical framework provide a shared system of values, meanings, and metaphors through which to organize the complexities of mind, behavior, relationships, and the therapeutic process itself. To illustrate the importance of theory as a way of sharing and building complex understandings, I would like to introduce you briefly to a few pieces that have been particularly helpful to me. I then explore and expand on these concepts more thoroughly in later chapters.

First, and foremost, is this idea of "learning from experience": learning who *you* can be in that room and what makes you help-ful or hurtful and how can you grow from these experiences. Bion (1991), echoing Freud, speaks of deepening the darkness to illu-minate the unseen. "Unless the obscurity can be circumvented," he says, "it will remain unobserved" (p. ix). We are always in the odd position of needing to be able to look over our own shoul-ders in order to try to see whatever we might be missing.

As an aside, or perhaps as a way of delving deeper inside, I would like to offer you a quote from Bion on the subject, which I find really delightful, not to mention reassuring. One thing I like about Bion is that he always seemed to be trying to step out of the way of his own shadow, so that people would not confuse him (as a person) with the message he was trying to convey. It's so easy for us to believe that someone else has the answers, but the other person can only point to his or her answers, and in the end we must find our own. So, here's the quote, from one of Bion's 1977 talks in New York. He says that it is only in prac-tice that

> you discover that it is worth your while talking to patients in the way that *you* talk to them—never mind whether it is sanctified by appearing in one of the Collected Works. That experience convinces you that it is worth while having some respect for your Self, for what you think and imagine and speculate. There is a curious kind of conviction about these occasions where what you say has an effect which is recognizably similar to your theo-ries. A "marriage" is taking place between you and you; a marriage between your thoughts and feelings (Bion, 1980, p. 27).

For Bion, our feelings—or "intuitions"—are quintessential clues toward the "truth" of our experiences. Bion was always talking about impossible things like "ultimate realities" and "truth instincts," and this would seem to be another of those impossible but completely essential things that Bion encourages us to think about: how to be ourselves and to find our own way with as much integrity and respect as we can muster. This was the challenge he set: to try to *be* as fully as possible in the moment, without regard to one's ideas about how or what one should or might be. This challenge becomes an invitation to our patients to enter into the dance, as well—to sound and resound into *their* own darkness.

The first challenge, then, is to be able to provide for ourselves a safe enough environment that we can *be* ourselves and utilize whatever resources might be available. This brings us to the crucial issue of containment. Bion's (1977) idea of the container and the contained goes beyond Winnicott's (1971) idea of the holding environment, although it lies in the same general direction. Crucial to Bion's conception is that he is talking about a recursive *relationship*. Whatever is contained also contains. So, at one level, we contain our patients and their distress by giving them a safe place to pull out their dirty laundry and sort through it with another human being who knows something about dirty laundry, because they have piles of it that *they* are always sorting through.

Thus, you provide the containment and you start to notice something interesting: that the containing you're doing is changing what's being contained, which is also changing that other container in the room, who is digesting and redefining meanings in turn.

This notion brings us to another level of containment, which has to do with signification processes and with meaning itself. In the process of being contained, meanings are being made and passed back and forth from one person to the other, and this relational processing becomes its own type of containment. It is a great relief to be able to share a common language with another person about important and troubling aspects of our worlds and beings. This capacity for sharing is built along with the relationship that we are building through our attempts to understand the other person and ourselves.

In many ways, the relationship is "the thing" in psychotherapy. It is the context in which change can happen, but it is also the "happening" itself. As we sit in the room together and try to find a way to communicate with one another, we begin to build a common language and a common history. In this process, we are constructing a scaffolding that we hope will hold us through whatever rough times may come. We are also constructing a model of a relationship.

At one level, we are building a model of a more adaptive type of relationship than the person has known, with new possibilities. At another level, we are building a model of the person's habitual modes of being in relationship, through which we can come to understand some of the difficulties this particular person encounters in interaction with others. The therapeutic relationship itself becomes a model of reality, which brings us to the idea of *myth*, Bion's term for metaphor.

3

Myth
Models of Reality

MYTH IS BION'S TERM for metaphor. They are interchangeable. What I like about the term myth is that it recognizes the power and the scope of the metaphor. Whole civilizations are captured within the myth. Whatever we call them, these metaphors become windows onto our realities and show us how these realities fit together; how they are configured. I call these configurations *patterns* (Charles, 2002a). Once you get away from the particulars and down to the level of structure, you start to see something really basic; something profoundly, awesomely simple at play.

A good example is Freud's (1900) conception of the Oedipus complex. In my early encounters with the idea of the Oedipus complex, it always seemed kind of flat and a little weird. Somehow, seeing a desire to have sex with my father as the ultimate epiphany that would open the doors of enlightenment just didn't do it for me. So I pushed it aside, because the idea just did not fit with the way my world seemed to be configured.

But then I find Bion (1977) talking about the Oedipus story as one of a series of myths, such as those of the Garden of Eden or the Tower of Babel, in which *knowing* is prohibited. Ah, I say, this sounds interesting. It invites me in to wonder about it, to sense the ripples of it—the layers.

We are always caught between surface and underlying meanings. If we don't get lost in the trappings, myth invites us to consider the complexities. For whatever reasons, Freud's use of the story of Oedipus did not invite me to discover the richness of the metaphor. Later theorists, however, as they unpacked some of the meanings for themselves, invited me to consider more deeply some of the layerings and potential meanings of this metaphor. Steiner (1985), for example, looks at this myth as a portrayal of *willful* blindness, in which the blindness is invoked as a means of not seeing one's own vulnerabilities. Steiner describes this as "turning a blind eye" (p. 161) to aspects of one's self and one's reality. In this way, he invites us to consider our complicity in not knowing aspects of reality that seem too terrible to know and also to consider the price of this avoidance.

If we think about the oedipal myth in terms of encounters with the forbidden—with whatever has seemed prohibited—we are invited to consider the feeling of prohibition itself: these edges beyond which we feel we must not go. Some of these warnings speak of real hazards—paths to be traversed carefully or not at all—whereas others speak more largely to our fears and our need to understand them so that we can travel with less strain. The prohibitions we encounter vary. Some have to do with knowledge per se, others with the more relational elements of growing up and making one's way in the world. (I discuss these types of prohibitions in greater detail in chapter 13.) The prohibitions may have to do with whether one can "come first" with either parent or whether one can know whatever has been deemed taboo in that family. In either case, we come up against what Lacan (1977) terms *the law*: the prohibitions that keep us safely within the bounds of culture.

However we view any specific prohibitions, myth invites us to consider more generally and also more deeply some of the enticements and prohibitions we encounter in being human. Whether encountered in classical forms or in current portrayals, the myth gives us a picture we can hold in mind. This picture offers a continuing reference point, enabling us to play more freely with subtleties and potential meanings. The narrative form provides an anchor—a way of not getting lost—not only within ourselves but also with the other. We can share the metaphor, build it, deconstruct it, rebuild it, try it on for size. Perhaps most important, we can share it—and re-share it. Like a vivid dream, it becomes a reference point to which we can return. It marks the place.

Speaking of marking the place, there are several metaphors that I would like to talk about more explicitly. I find these metaphors extremely useful to have in mind in this work, because they mark important places and help get us out of tough spots (which, in turn, makes it easier for us to jump—or maybe just ease tentatively—*into* some of the tough spots through which we need to find our way).

The first metaphor is W.R. Bion's (1977) notion of *container* and *contained*, which I touched on briefly in chapter 2. The second originated with Klein (1946) in her descriptions of a progression from what she terms a *paranoid–schizoid* position, in which reality is fragmented, to a *"depressive"* position, in which oppositions can be contained. Bion then transforms this conceptualization by taking it out of a linear frame and focusing on the interactive relationship between the two positions. The third metaphor I consider is Klein's (1946, 1952) conceptualization of *projective identification*. I look at these metaphors in greater depth in the following chapters.

4

Container and Contained

THE INTERRELATED NOTION OF the *container* and the *contained* is a fundamental metaphor to have in mind as we try to make ourselves comfortable within the therapeutic space. As mentioned previously, this conceptualization marks the important interplay between whatever is being held and whatever is doing the holding. It also marks the fact that ideas and feelings are dynamic and depend on the contexts in which they are considered. In clinical practice, people come to us precisely because their problems seem unmanageable. Our first task then is to be able to contain their fear through our own hope. We base this hope on previous experiences in which our persistence has paid off and there has been substantive change and real relief.

The notions of container and contained may be seen as a relational way of viewing what have been termed more generally *frame* issues. Langs (1979), most particularly, noted the importance of attending to the ground rules and framework of the therapeutic environment as a way of understanding the process. The consulting room is a bounded space in which rules, regularities, and deviations have fundamental meanings. There are various strictures and injunctions that we come upon in learning this work: "rules" as to what might be deemed good or bad, permissible or forbidden.

In my experience, it is important to be able to see these rules as permeable boundaries that have come into being for important reasons but must be applied or set aside mindfully. These rules provide useful warnings and guideposts marking potentially treacherous territory. They warn us up front as to the difficulties that might be encountered should we set them aside. Warning does not mean, however, that we should see these strictures as absolute limits. It does mean that we should be prepared for a challenge when we dare to move into murky or treacherous waters.

An easy example is time. Time limits bound the session in useful ways. There are times, however, when this type of limit may get in the way. If we are stringent in enforcing these limits, they are less problematic. If we are too rigid, however, we may lose some important sources of information. For example, in chapter 8, I discuss the case of a woman for whom the time limits had very entrenched meanings. The difficulties we encountered in keeping the sessions bounded opened up an avenue for discussing pivotal issues in terms of how this woman viewed herself in relation to others. It provided a vehicle for beginning to tease apart some of the extremely condensed realities (*symbolic equations* [see chaps. 7 and 8]) that were at play but that had not previously been accessible to conscious awareness.

Bion (1977) adds an extremely useful parameter to ideas of the frame through his ideas about the container and the contained. This conceptualization extends Loewald's (1951) observations regarding the generative interplay between ego and reality. As we note more pointedly that boundaries affect whatever is being bounded and vice versa, we are aided in setting aside some of our rigid ideas about rules. This enhanced flexibility affords us greater perspective from which to begin to think about our rules more explicitly and to be mindful of them rather than to be reflexively reactive.

As we try to understand the therapeutic space, the first issue is that of containment itself: How do we create a space in which constructive work may take place? This preliminary containment poses particular challenges for the novice clinician, who has little experience on which to base her hope and so tends to feel self-conscious about her status and potential. This heightened self-consciousness can make it difficult to find one's place within the room. Containment, in this sense, involves titrating our own anxiety enough to be able to attend more pointedly to the needs, feelings, and experience of the other person.

The first obstacle is the implicit belief that we should have answers, even though we inevitably begin a treatment in the dark. The new clinician believes that this is a function of inexperience but then begins to understand that it is merely a part of the process and an important part at that. This not knowing can also be seen as a mark of respect for the task that lies ahead. After all, if the problem were really so simple, it is likely that the person would have solved it already. One of the advantages we gain with experience is a greater ease with the knowledge that we don't know where we are going—or exactly how we are going to get there. We learn to be more comfortable with the inevitability of not knowing and can then more easily proceed on our path of learning to know whatever might be important to understand in the moment.

This idea of "learning to know" invites us to grapple more explicitly with the paradoxes we often face in psychoanalytic work. Bion (1967a), for example, cautions us to avoid memory or desire, the implication being that we should not foreclose on whatever we might be able to discover as long as our preconceptions, desires, and fears do not get in the way. From Bion's perspective, we are continually having to set aside what we *think* we know so that we might actually learn something. "To this end," he says, "the function of the interpretation should be such that the transition from *knowing about* reality to *becoming real* is furthered" (Bion, 1965, p. 153). If we take this idea seriously, it helps us to sit through the silences and trust in the process. One of the paradoxes in this work is that we need to be able to have hope in a generic sense and yet also be mindful that even well-intentioned hopes or narrowly defined ideas about health, dis-order, or being helpful can get in the way of coming to grips with the other person's needs, desires, and values.

In order to have any really useful ideas about where we should be heading in the work, we need to be able to be present with the person in the moment and develop a sense of the world as they see and experience it. This attunement requires sufficient containment of our own needs and fears so that we can shift our attention from these to whatever the other person might be feel-ing. Then we can also begin to notice that there is a growing awareness that takes place within us as we continue to work with the person week after week. This emerging familiarity—this sense of pattern or order—helps to titrate our anxiety, particularly if we can keep our minds on trying to understand rather than try-ing to be helpful. It also helps to reassure the other person and encourages him to take his own needs, feelings, and experiences more seriously.

The more understanding there is in the room, the greater the containment. As our anxiety decreases, the other person is better able to borrow on some of our faith. Our willingness to sit with what we do not know seems to provide a floor to the other person's anxieties and helps to keep the affect from spiraling and intensifying to the point where we are merely reenacting a trau-matic moment. At times the person may need this intensifica-tion in order to provide us with a lived sense of how powerful their negative affect can be. At times, however, this type of reen-actment serves little purpose and merely retraumatizes the indi-vidual. The crucial piece of this process is to be able to encounter the moment and try to learn something from it. If we are will-ing to be clear within ourselves as to what we do and do not yet know, we can begin to try to fill in the blanks, to answer the real questions, which only become apparent if we are willing to enter-tain them. I'll explore this issue in greater depth later in this chapter as we examine the case of Ruth.

This filling up the spaces that we do to avoid being aware of not knowing is what Bion (1977) calls "saturating" the space. I find this idea useful. It signifies a kind of deadly containment with no room for growth or change. Any space or concept that becomes saturated by what we think we know about it is no longer particularly useful because it cannot grow. Saturated ideas lose their plasticity. They become flat and stagnant. So, for example, if we have a closed set of ideas about what being a therapist is, we're stuck either being that or being wrong, without really having an opportunity to learn for ourselves, from our own experience, what being a therapist might be.

Our need to find anchors—and signposts to guide our way—can make us jump too quickly on "meanings" as saturated elements that leave little room for growth. We tend to reify concepts so that they come to have the appearance of actual entities rather than merely marking a constellation of meanings that may come together in a particular kind of way. We do this with diagnoses, for example, forgetting that these labels are merely metaphors, a way of "marking the spot." If we can pull away from our ideas of a fixed "reality," we can better attend to whatever nuances, subtleties, and meanings might also become apparent in this particular reality. We can then use our terms as frames of reference rather than being used by them.

The importance of being able to experience the lived moment cannot be stressed too highly. Many of our patients come to us so out of touch with self, other, and world that knowledge per se may have little value unless it can be joined with an actual lived experience. Winnicott (1971), for example, notes how important it is to be able to have a new experience in order to make the possibility of change real and palpable. We must be able to be more present in a particular moment in order to discover it more fully and to better discern its potential. This being in the moment requires a sufficient sense of safety to enable us to be present with one another, no mean task. The intimacy of engaging with another being at a deep level can be terrifying!

As we consider the issue of containment and how we might make the therapeutic space sufficiently safe for ourselves and our patients, some very useful notions to have in mind are Winnicott's (1965) conceptions of the "good-enough" mother who provides for the child a "holding" or "facilitating" environment within which to grow. These ideas came from his observations of mothers and young children. Winnicott, a pediatrician as well as a psychoanalyst, was an astute observer of his tiny patients and their relationships with their parents. He had noticed that if the mother was good enough, the child was able to develop his or her own resources, using the mother as a safety net.

Winnicott applies these ideas directly to the therapeutic environment. In his own work, he explicitly attempted to provide a safe place within which the patient could develop his or her own resources. An important aspect of this safety is having respect for the process itself. Our fears of not being good enough, of not having enough to offer, can cause us to foreclose on the important containing processes that are developing between the patient and ourselves. Our lack of faith then provides a model of fear-driven foreclosure that further affirms the other's lack of faith in self and world (Charles, 2003).

Winnicott (1971) was keenly aware of the hazards of pre-empting the patient's developing faculties through premature or excessive interpretations, suggesting that "the patient's creativity can only too easily be stolen by a therapist who knows too much" (p. 57). For Winnicott, as for Bion, the process of becoming one's self is much more important than "receiving" knowledge. Moreover, receiving knowledge can impede our ability to learn to use our own resources. As we defer to the other's sensibilities rather than fine-tuning our own, we lose touch with important information as to what constitutes safety, comfort, and pleasure for us in our world. Self-reference is then replaced by attempts to apply arbitrary values or standards that might or might not hold true.

Let me give you an example. I worked for some time with a young woman who had learned to discount her own perspective, her own mind. Kate, the third of five children, was the only daughter in a household in which females were devalued, sexualized, and ridiculed. Feelings, in particular, were pathologized and devalued, as were Kate's passionate curiosity and thirst for knowledge. In this environment, Kate's emotions, rather than being useful to her in their signal functions, had become a sign of deficiency and a source of humiliation. She had become unable to use either her thinking or her feeling as sources of information without feeling subject to attack. Her fear had left her utterly immobilized.

In the early days of our work together, when I asked Kate how she felt about something, she would initially be at a loss. She would then think of someone in her world who might have an opinion on the subject and would proceed to tell me how that person viewed her. Initially I found this behavior quite perplexing. Over time, I came to appreciate how strikingly this woman privileged any other person's perspective over her own. I was aware, however, that Kate also cherished a more positive image of herself, hidden deep inside.

A person whose needs and feelings have been overridden by caregivers often learns that survival depends on keeping the overt focus on the other rather than on the self (see Fairbairn, 1952; Guntrip, 1989). Such thinking keeps the self from coming under attack but also keeps the person from developing a sense of efficacy and potency in the world. By refusing to reveal the self, she preserves it but also affirms her lack of faith in its viability. The act of hiding comes to affirm the sense of devaluation. This double bind is very difficult to overcome, as the very means for survival (keeping the self hidden) precludes growth and adaptation. Very often, in psychoanalytic work, we discover that the humiliating secret that the person has guarded so carefully is a function of having been attacked rather than of any real incapacity. The real incapacity that results is an inability to be aware of and respectfully attend to one's own needs.

In cases such as these, the at-risk self is made safe (contained) by taking care of the other but at the price of its own growth and development. In this way, containment of negative affect comes to mean taking care of the other's needs and feelings rather than more explicitly focusing on the self. We can see that containment can be a slippery concept. It matters what is being contained and for whom and the relative price for each. Using as his model Klein's ideas about projective identification (which I explore in chapter 8), Bion (1977) explores in depth the relationship between the container and whatever is being contained. What he finds, most pointedly, is that each fundamentally affects the other.

In the instance just presented, we can surmise that Kate had learned to contain her own affect by ensuring her parents' well-being. In turn, she had learned to attune herself to others as a way of safeguarding her own well-being. Although this stance helped to keep her relatively safe, it also kept her profoundly out of touch with her own needs and feelings. In our early work together, I refused to arbitrarily privilege the perspective of the other (including my own) but rather encouraged a closer attention to whatever signs we could discern of what Kate herself might be feeling or thinking. At times, Kate would become irritated by what she felt was a withholding of insight on my part. Over time, however, she was able to appreciate the positive aspects of this withholding.

As Kate grew more aware of her own frame of reference without feeling attacked by me for doing so, her anxieties over knowing her self and feelings came to be more contained. Part of this titration process consisted of being able to understand the anxiety in a different way. Rather than reading her arousal as a sign of imminent danger, Kate learned to interpret it as an indication that she was coming upon territory that had always *seemed* dangerous but was not inherently unmanageable. Kate's emerging insight provided some containment for her anxiety as she breached the inhibition against attending to her needs and feelings. This opening made the whole idea of knowing self seem less dangerous and less inaccessible.

Kate describes her mother as extremely narcissistic, unable to attune herself to her daughter's needs and feelings. Rather, she appears to have become either distressed or angry when Kate would express her own needs. Optimally, the mother contains the child's distress. However, when the parent's needs become primary, the child often learns to be vigilant to the needs of the parent and to titrate the parent's distress, even at the expense of his or her own well-being. For the child, the parent's well-being is so integral to her own that it becomes paramount (Fairbairn, 1952).

Even when the mother does try to keep the child's affect within tolerable bounds, she is also being affected by the containing process itself. As she moderates the child's tension, she is taking it in. If she cannot manage it herself, it will spill over into the relationship, creating further tension in the child. This tension, however, is likely to be experienced more pointedly as "other" even though it seems to originate in the child. In this small example, we can see how complex it becomes to separate out one person's affect from another's in an intimate relationship. This dynamic interplay is often denoted by the term *affective field*.

The affective field is a palpable reality in the moment. It is experienced by each participant in his or her own way. When we speak of the patient's affective resonance, we call it *transference*. When we speak of the therapist's affective resonance, we call it *countertransference*. This terminology clearly privileges the therapist's experience, which is depicted as being responsive to what the patient brings rather than as originating more specifically in the therapist him- or herself. However, our reactions to others are inevitably patterned in accord with our previous experiences and expectations (Solms, 1996; Charles, 2002a).

In spite of the tendency to privilege the therapist's view, we can see how failures in the therapist's containing functions (in the sense of being able to track and to manage his or her own affect) can leak into the treatment, much as we described in the relationship between parent and child. This hazard makes it particularly important for the therapist to be able to track her own affect through countertransference reactions, so that she can help the patient make sense of what is going on. Failures to acknowledge affect can result in a game of "hot potato," in which more energy is put into disowning than understanding.

Ideas about countertransference have been quite varied. Countertransference was originally framed by Freud (1910) as a relatively pathological or at least problematic response on the part of the therapist that should be overcome. Over time, conceptions have evolved to view countertransference as the entire constellation of affective responses of the therapist, configured according to his or her own patterns of experience in much the same way as transference might be viewed. From this framework, countertransference provides important information that the therapist can utilize in making sense of whatever is happening in the room. I take up the topic of countertransference in greater detail in chapter 12.

At this point, suffice it to say that our affective signals are particularly important in psychoanalytic work, in which meanings are layered and the words themselves may not tell us the whole story. Nonverbal aspects such as tone, prosody, and gesture can all profoundly affect the meaning of a given communication. As Bion (1977) notes, it is also important to be able to consider the uses to which any particular statement or behavior is being put. The same phrase can have very different meanings depending on the context and the purpose being served (see

Charles, 2002b). In the moment, our affective resonance may be the best marker of meaning.

At times, it is most important to have a sense of where we are headed; of whether we are moving in the direction of greater understanding or of evasion. Being able to mark these directions helps us to wonder more directly about the conditions under which learning is enhanced or foreclosed. We need to be able to get our bearings within the nonverbal domains in order to be able to provide sufficient containment that growth might occur.

Let me give you an example that shows the importance, but also some of the difficulties, of providing containment in the consulting room. We tend to think of containment in terms of providing emotional support, often our primary relationship-building tool. However, that particular type of containment is not always the first order of the day. For someone for whom contact has been dangerous or abrasive, containment may mean learning to tolerate the discomfort of encountering one another. With Ruth, for example, my ability to tolerate her reactivity and the chaos she experienced in our relationship helped me to begin to understand her predicament. It was this growing understanding that validated her experience sufficiently to provide her with a sense of containment and support.

In my work with Ruth, containment was the crucial preliminary issue in the treatment. She had come in very explicitly looking for someone who might understand her concerns and take them seriously after several failed treatments in which this recognition had not occurred. She had little hope that this might be possible but had accepted the referral from her doctor in the off chance that I might be able to help her. She was not, however, remotely optimistic and set about with quite fierce determination to let me know exactly what had gone wrong in previous treatments lest she waste her time and crush her hopes once again.

It was difficult at first to understand exactly what it was that Ruth was looking for. Her presenting problem was her inability to paint, which had resulted from a breakdown that had occurred several decades before, when she was in her early twenties. Ruth seemed, on the surface, to function quite well. She was bright and articulate and able to earn a living teaching. She was not, however, able to paint, which troubled her deeply. It was not clear what frightened her more—the prospect of never painting again or of losing touch with her desire to do so. In an odd way, her very ability to be happy and contented with her life posed the greatest threat to what she held most precious. Her focus on contentment had been the danger that ultimately had driven her from previous treatments. Her therapists' inability to understand the dire nature of her dilemma had led to an impasse in each treatment. Being understood and taken seriously was the crucial issue in Ruth's agenda. Without this basic acknowledgment, there was no containment of her anxiety, which at times reached immobilizing proportions.

How this issue manifested in our work together was as an almost unendurable urgency on Ruth's part to have me understand her dilemma. The urgency was such that my own sense that I indeed understood did not make even a ripple in Ruth's presentation. There ensued many long months of unrelenting waves of earnest entreaties, in which Ruth would tell me the history of her attempts to make previous therapists understand The Problem. My work during this arduous time consisted of sufficiently containing my own distress that I could provide an environment in which Ruth could continue to tell me her story. The fact that I thought I understood became irrelevant except insofar as Ruth could sense my understanding and attain some measure of comfort as a result. However, even as she began to relax her guard, the wall would go up once again. She had no wish to be fooled by any presumption of understanding and so would redouble her efforts and remind me yet again of The Problem and the history of its not being understood.

As time went on and I became better able to tolerate these assaults and contain them within myself, the therapeutic space became one in which overwhelming affect could be titrated and diminished to manageable proportions. At an experiential level, ideas were being exchanged as to whether Ruth was utterly beyond understanding or assisting and, at a deeper level, whether she really had any value at all. One fear underneath the incredible assaultiveness of her presentation was that her previous therapists, who had suggested she just "give up her dreams and go on disability," had been right and that it was Ruth's dreams of artistic productivity that were the problem. Deeply hidden within Ruth's armor was the terrifying image of herself as a crazy old bag lady, a deluded fool with visions of grandeur. The fact that I could encounter her as a person of value helped her to believe in her own hopes and dreams.

Our impasses are often worked through by way of reenactments. Ruth had invited me into a reenactment of the impasse she had experienced with previous caregivers. Taking stock of my own experiences of being with Ruth, I conjectured that the previous communication failures had resulted, not from Ruth's inability to communicate, but rather from her previous therapists' frustration at their inability to soothe her and to thereby stop the assaults on themselves. Their inability to tolerate her distress or their own had resulted in frustrating and disconfirming attempts to stop Ruth (and thereby themselves) from "feeling bad." In contrast, my ability to tolerate my own distress in the presence of Ruth's intense negative affect enabled us to talk about our experiences in interaction with one another. This acknowledgment and affirmation of her reality as she experienced it provided the initial containment Ruth required in order to begin to tolerate her distress rather than merely to relieve mine at her own expense.

Breaking the old pattern in this way helped us to relieve the affective intensity sufficiently that we could begin to consider alternative meanings. The reduced intensity helped provide sufficient grounding that we could begin to distinguish between her fear and the thoughts that had become linked to it. Distinguishing between the feeling and the meanings enabled us to consider alternative meanings in a way that further contained the anxiety. As Ruth began to affirm these alternate meanings in her interactions outside the consulting room, she learned that she could contain her *own* anxiety as well, which was a major achievement and a further source of containment of the fears that were linked to her self-disparagement.

As the incredible intensity of the affect began to be contained, we began to be able to inhabit together a space in which ideas could be exchanged. Ruth was then able to make use of some of my observations. These reflections provided further containment, as they affirmed for her that I was, indeed, taking her seriously and, moreover, that I had some ideas as to why she found herself in the dilemmas she described. Although Ruth often found it difficult to understand my views or to believe that they might be true, the idea that there might be another perspective gave her hope.

Over time, I began to understand that Ruth's vehemence in countering my views did not reflect her unwillingness to see things from my perspective but rather her inability to do so. This awareness helped me to persist in my beliefs in a way that helped Ruth eventually to be able to understand them. We began to see that my way of looking at things, because it was so different from hers, inspired acute anxiety in her, which manifested as attacks on my thoughts. Ruth needed me to be able to survive these attacks (in Winnicott's [1971] terms, she needed to be able to destroy the object and have it survive, see chapter 7) in order to begin to be able to "play" with these new ideas I was putting forth.

I continued to interpret to Ruth my understanding of the interpersonal field in which she was caught and how it had come to be set up in such an unsatisfying way. Over time, this new perspective helped her to begin to understand the dilemma in which she has become caught with her mother, and which she now played out in other important relationships as well. As we attempted to understand what had gone wrong in Ruth's early life, it appeared that her mother had become overwhelmed by the daughter's distress, which made her utterly unavailable as a source of comfort. Ruth had experienced her mother's distress as rejection and had read this rejection as a sign that she was repugnant. Whenever she would try to engage with her mother around a difficult issue (more generally, anything of importance to Ruth), her mother would withdraw. Ruth would then redouble her efforts to engage her mother, which only increased the mother's withdrawal and the daughter's distress.

This same pattern played out in other relationships as well. When Ruth encountered a lack of understanding in another person, she would feel compelled to push for understanding. However, she was not good at understanding where the other person had become stuck. She lived in a world in which all others seemed to have the answers; she alone had not been given the key. She experienced herself as deficient and isolated in a world of omniscient, withholding others.

Ruth's compulsion for acknowledgment had an intensity that could be unnerving and distancing. The early years of our work together had felt like a barrage in which Ruth raged at me about her distress over not being understood. The rage was ostensibly directed at previous individuals who had not understood her, but she could not really imagine that I might understand her either.

My urgency to reassure Ruth came in part from my urgency to relieve this onslaught I was experiencing in each session. Extrapolating from my own feelings in being with her, I presumed that many of the reactions she had received from previous therapists had come from their own inability to tolerate the magnitude of the barrage. What she tended to encounter, then, was either outright rejection, compassionate condescension, or real compassion that Ruth was not able to take in in any beneficial way. The compassion was often accompanied by misguided attempts to calm Ruth down that minimized the very distress that she was attempting to have validated. This lack of recognition seemed to be the impasse in which she had found herself in her previous therapies.

The key ingredient that had kept relationships frustrating was Ruth's idea that the other person would be able to understand if only she could explain it well enough. This had not been true in her relationship with her mother nor in her relationship with her previous therapists. It did, however, seem to be true in her relationship with me. As she was able to communicate her dilemma to me and have the dilemma acknowledged, she was able also to see that there could be relational failures that were not "her fault." This notion became a pivotal turning point in the treatment. It introduced, for Ruth, the idea that she would need to take into account the other person's relative capacities in interaction rather than assuming that any deficit was inevitably her own. This idea provided her with a way of containing her own distress in moments of impasse with others. Her ability to titrate her own discomfort helped to relieve the escalating cycle and to reduce the other's distress in turn.

As the interpersonal field began to be conceptualized as one in which she might carry equal weight and value, Ruth began to be able to make profound inroads in her interpersonal world. Her enhanced ability to interact with others also helped her to achieve some successes in creative endeavors that had been inaccessible for a very long time. Creativity requires the ability to provide ourselves with sufficient containment that we are able to tolerate the lack of appreciation by the other. Sustaining this containment has been a continuing struggle in our work together. Ruth is finally beginning to be able to envision ways of sustaining it for herself and bringing her creativity more fully into being.

5

Symptoms
Marking the Spot

AMBIVALENCE IS A powerful force. We are always caught between the desire to know and the desire to not know. Symptoms may be seen as a way of marking something important that we have not been able to more constructively manage or work through. The symptom provides us with a way of remembering without forcing an awareness that might be overwhelming. It marks the spot.

There are some experiences that are difficult for us to know about in words, perhaps because the event occurred quite early, before the advent of verbal symbolic language, or because the event was too traumatic to be able to encode in this form. Overwhelming affect makes it difficult to organize our experience, so that traumatic memories tend to be encoded at the sensory-motor level, as body-memories or "symptoms" (Person and Klar, 1994).

Our ability to make sense of primary experience is built through our early relationships with caregivers. In these relationships, the attunement of the other person helps us to make sense of the multitude of nonverbal meanings that affect us without our necessarily being explicitly aware of them. "Good-enough" parenting involves reciprocal interactions through which one develops the sense of being understood and therefore of being understandable in a positive sense. The caregiver's attunement helps the child make the transition from a reliance on the other for affect regulation to a greater reliance on the self. In this process, the child is also learning a basic sense of trust in self and world, from which hope—and with it frustration tolerance—can be built.

The reciprocal relationship between the mother (as container) and the child (who feels "contained" by the mother) has obvious parallels in the therapeutic relationship. In many ways, we need to be sufficiently available to our patients to enable them to grow. If we take up too much space, they get lost in the shuffle; if we take up too little space, they may feel abandoned or overwhelmed by affective experiences they cannot manage on their own. If we can titrate the affect sufficiently that they can experience it without becoming overwhelmed in the process, they can better learn from their own experience. In this way, we are also instilling faith in self and, with it, hope for the future.

We hope, then, to provide an environment that feels safe enough that the person can begin to get their bearings sufficiently to be able even to consider where they might want to go from there. If we see the goal of therapy as greater understanding, we want to be able to use as many resources as possible to further that understanding. One of our most important resources is our affect, which we learn to read as a signal that continually provides feedback about our emotional status at any given moment. If we are able to notice our affect at relatively low levels, we can act accordingly and can generally keep our affect within comfortable limits. From this state of relative equilibrium, we are better able to register and utilize spikes of affect as signals telling us that something is wrong and requires our attention.

This signaling system is extremely valuable when it is functioning properly. It helps us to mark pleasurable and unpleasurable experiences and to organize an understanding of where and how these are encountered. Overwhelming affect, however, impedes the cognitive processes required in order to make sense of and organize our experience (LeDoux, 1999). Affect that is not kept within tolerable limits is extremely stressful and overwhelms our systems, often resulting in avoidant maneuvers of one sort or another to reduce the traumatic impact of the affective onslaught (van der Kolk, 1987; Krystal, 1988). At the extreme, individual affects cease to be useful in their signal functions, and affect itself becomes a signal invoking avoidant strategies.

This type of pattern is particularly problematic with fear reactions, which become entrenched very easily. Because of their inherent survival value, fear reactions are extremely difficult to overcome (LeDoux, 2002). Fear can lead to the types of avoidant and ineffective coping strategies—such as depersonalization and substance abuse—associated with deficits in affect differentiation and self-care (Krystal, 1988).

For example, substance abuse may be seen as a maladaptive attempt to devise an external "cause" for intrapsychic pain and feelings of unreality. It creates a sleight of hand in which the actual problem—the underlying pain—gets lost beneath the more apparent problem: the substance use. This type of sleight of hand is an important characteristic of symptoms. Although we often need to attend to the overt symptom, if we fail to also attend to the underlying distress, the distress is likely to reappear in this or some other form.

We tend to overvalue symptoms; to see them as The Problem rather than as signs of an underlying problem. This tendency is exacerbated by a mental health system that reflects our own urges to identify problems as a way of reassuring ourselves that we can solve them. This type of foreclosure is one place where we can clearly see our ambivalence at play. Real change is hard won. There is always a part of our patients (and ourselves) that would be pleased to give up arduous work in favor of a simpler and more easily defined solution.

In this regard, it is important to have ideas about what it is we think we are doing in this work. Solving problems is a useful endeavor. Although it occurs in all therapy, in psychodynamic therapies it is not the ultimate goal. Rather, the goal of psychodynamic treatment may be seen as encouraging reflection that can lead to understanding. This understanding then leads to an enhanced ability to more adaptively solve one's own problems as they arise. If we can learn to pay closer attention to ourselves and our interactions, we can learn a great deal that is useful in making our way in the world.

It is important to know what our goals are so that we are better able to think about the extent to which our goals are in line with, or in opposition to, those of the people with whom we work. Too often, a failure to examine and explore explicit versus implicit goals can result in an impasse in which we find ourselves playing out one side or the other of our patients' ambivalence rather than helping them to explore it.

Bion (1977) pointed to the crucial distinction between efforts toward evasion and efforts toward understanding. In his later theorizing, he spoke of a *truth instinct* (Grotstein, 2002). I call it *integrity*. Whatever term we use, we are alluding to an internal reference point that marks these forks in the road we come to, where it is only our essential integrity or instinct for truth that helps to provide markers distinguishing the path of growth from the path of avoidance.

We come to these choice points often in our work, moments when we might choose the more difficult path or avoid it and try to pretend to ourselves that such avoidance is acceptable. Such moments of what Sartre called "bad faith" are palpable. They have their impact. The lie is a particularly problematic choice to make in our role as therapist, for then we communicate to the other person that risks are best not taken and that lying can be concealed. Part of our job as therapists is to help our patients (and ourselves) to believe that they might actually take the path of truth without facing imminent annihilation.

Let me give you an example. I worked with a man whose relationships with self and other might best be captured by the term *schizoid*. Erik's relationships were few and impoverished, and he tended to feel powerless, alienated, and persecuted by others. His speech was rambling and tangential and I often found myself lost. It was hard for me to know, in the moment, whether I was lost because of some defect in my attention or whether, indeed, he was not making sense. In the moment, I would want to cover over the gap. My urge would be to try to make sense of whatever was there; to "catch up"; to figure out what it was he had been talking about. I would find myself pretending I was not lost, hoping (much like David in chapter 9) to make the lie true by "finding him" once again.

Initially, the endeavor seemed legitimate, but I began to notice that it had an odd effect on the treatment. If I did not own up to the gap, the distance between us was not repaired and became larger and more palpable. An opportunity clearly had been lost. If I did own up to my lostness, however, the admission seemed to repair the gap. We could find one another and continue on our way. The relationship seemed strengthened and the work deepened in the process. Over time, this process of disruption and repair became something that we could talk about and that further helped us to mark the importance of meeting difficult truths without turning away.

Such moments of disruption and potential repair have been described by Beebe and Lachmann (1988, 1994, 1998) as fundamental turning points in relationships. Moments of disruption can be extremely disorganizing, particularly when we are faced with a lack of responsiveness or recognition in the face of the other (Tronick, 1989). Alternatively, with appropriate acknowledgment, these disruptions potentially lead to what Beebe and Lachmann term *heightened affective moments*, and Stern and his colleagues (1998a,b) describe as *moments of meeting*. These moments of engagement have tremendous potential within our work.

Acknowledgment of Erik's implicit perceptions helped him to take these perceptions more seriously. Although he thought of himself as very out of touch with others, he actually did resonate to nonverbal elements in the affective field. In his family, however, acknowledging these elements had been taboo; it was unacceptable to be aware of uncomfortable feelings and to speak of them. The conflict between knowing and not knowing resulted in increasing agitation as affect intensified. The consulting room provided us with an opportunity to more explicitly track and organize the perceptual cues that he had responded to affectively but had not been able to more explicitly recognize and name.

Erik discovered that in the therapeutic relationship it was acceptable to be aware of uncomfortable feelings and it was not forbidden to speak of them. Being able to acknowledge and speak about uncomfortable realities helped to affirm for Erik that he was neither so lost nor so lacking in resources as he had imagined. What he was in need of were opportunities to validate his perceptions so that he could strengthen and build on them. Being able to recognize and differentiate his own affective signals helped Eric make sense of them rather than merely avoid such feelings.

Another issue that often comes up in reference to the symptom is the interplay between the literal and the metaphorical reality. Staying within the bounds of concrete, pragmatic reality can make us feel a bit more comfortable—a bit better grounded—but it can also keep us from making any real movement in the work. In contrast to Ruth, who very explicitly did not want me to confuse the symptom with The Problem, many individuals take the opposite position. One way in which this issue presents itself in the room can be through a diagnostic label that comes to have such a pragmatic reality that it is difficult to consider it as something that might mask other meanings.

For example, people at times talk about their depression as though it were a concrete entity that takes over and holds them in its grip for no apparent reason. Although depression is often experienced in this way, it also has meanings, causes, and connections with the person's history and experiences of self and world. It is in being willing to explore those connections that the person can begin to have a greater understanding and thereby greater control over the symptoms associated with the depression.

Although this type of diagnostic entity often has physiological aspects that the person may or may not choose to relieve through physiological means, there are always psychological factors at play. As therapists, our portion of the work is to help the person to be able to think through the possibilities and potential consequences of intervening at one level or another and then to come to some agreement as to how therapy might be useful. In this way, individuals who come to us ostensibly "suffering from a debilitating disease," such as Attention Deficit Disorder (ADD) or Bipolar Disorder, may be helped to understand how looking beyond the idea of disorder to the possible meanings of their symptoms might help to ameliorate the symptoms.

People vary in terms of their disposition to view psychological distress as psychologically or physiologically determined. This diversity makes it important to be able to consider and clarify differences in perspective between patient and therapist and to think about how we might best work within the parameters dictated by the other person's worldview. For example, I have worked with individuals who have been labeled *bipolar* who found medications helpful and sought therapy as an adjunct to their medication. Others, in contrast, found the medications more problematic and were seeking psychological assistance as a means of reducing their dependence on medications. Whatever our perspective, it is beneficial to have an understanding of our own idiosyncratic reactions to stress and of those factors that exacerbate or reduce internal and external stressors. Keeping in mind the other person's perspective helps us to provide information in ways that are most likely to be useful and beneficial (see McWilliams, 2003, for a discussion of the educative aspects of treatment).

Our definitions play an important role in our psychological well-being. This is a sphere in which the difference between normal and dysfunctional tends to be a matter of degree rather than of disjunction. As a result, the meanings we attribute to a given symptom can be a pivotal factor in the exacerbation or reduction of distress. This issue can be particularly important when the person has a symptom that they define in such a way that the definition becomes more problematic than the symptom itself. This dilemma often occurs in relation to dissociative symptoms, in which the very nature of the symptom marks a point of alienation.

For example, for many people, "hearing voices" marks an internal dialogue that is experienced as "other" and yet the person's reality testing is clearly intact. In such cases, the person's alarm at this indicator of "pathology" exacerbates whatever stressors they are already experiencing. It is then important for the therapist to be able to contextualize the symptom in terms of a normative model as to how we distance ourselves from our distress. Being able to see the symptom as a normative mode of maintaining equilibrium carried to an uncomfortable extreme can help people to get their bearings and thereby alleviate some of the anxiety. As the anxiety over the symptom abates, we are then in a better position to attempt to understand the symptom itself.

Symptoms are an important means for calling to our attention an aspect of experience that has been unresolved and continues to be a source of distress. Although our terms and labels can offer the illusion of consensus, actual meanings can be highly individualized. For example, at one point in our work together, Thomas expressed concerns that he might have an attention deficit. This concern came from his tendency to be anxious and distractible and to become preoccupied by obsessive thoughts. Designated a "gifted" child early in childhood, Thomas had never really been able to live up to his promise and had developed a view of himself in which important aspects seemed to be missing. Eventually this idea of deficit crystallized under the rubric of ADD. This attention deficit—this inability to concentrate—became a cover story that obscured facts that he was hiding from himself about ways in which his parents had failed him over the years.

In Thomas's household, his mother's own limits had provided the constraints that defined what could be tolerated and what could be known. The most important fact to *not* know was anything that might point to his mother in blame. Accommodating to his mother's reality was essential to psychic survival in this family, and Thomas had learned to be a master of the game. When he would move outside of the accepted limits, his mother would become enraged and Thomas would be sent to his room. He rarely had any idea of what he had done wrong, and he learned to create fantasies in his room as a way of passing the time and also of changing the subject. In this way, he was able to retain control in his internal world while feeling very out of control in the world at large.

Thomas now prides himself on his ability to play with ideas, to turn them over and around like some grand Rubik's cube awaiting deciphering. And yet, he also has come to realize that the game itself is a deception that covers his ambivalence. He plays out this game as a way of avoiding knowing about the puzzle he would and would not like to solve. This puzzle has to do with uncomfortable details regarding relationships within his family, how aspects of self may or may not be valued, and the various prices he pays for knowing versus not knowing.

As we have explored the meanings of Thomas's symptoms over time, he has been less willing to view them as "the problem." Instead, he has learned to use his symptoms as a signal that something is wrong and needs his attention. He no longer accepts his anxiety-laced ideas about dangers in the external world as facts needing to be solved and can recognize the pattern of guilt and danger as a sign that he has not been attending to his own internal needs. Rather than seeing his preoccupations as signs of an attentional deficit, he can register the distractibility as a sign of his distress. Marking the distress in this way helps to legit-imize Thomas's needs and feelings and to titrate the panic that rises when his needs conflict with those of another. As he becomes less frightened of affirming his own perspective, he is better able to organize his perceptions and to utilize the distress as a signal directing him to attend to his own needs and feelings. He can take his own well-being into consideration rather than reflexively deferring to the needs of the other.

Initially, Thomas was so certain that something was wrong with him that he would read any disturbance in the affective field as a sign that he had done something wrong that would result in dire retribution. Seeing the other person's responsibil-ity in an encounter would result in anxiety and the sense that something was wrong with him. "You have this idea that some-thing must be wrong with whatever it is you are doing," I told him. "If it's worth having, it must be out of reach, and there seems to be something wrong with getting something you might really want."

Because he was not supposed to be the frame of reference, Thomas had the idea that the fact that his mind often wandered was a problem rather than perhaps a sign of conflicting demands or of creativity. He seemed to feel as though following his own direction was a violation of some basic rule. One day he told me that he had been reading a book but that his mind kept wan-dering. "I keep wandering off into these other ideas."

"You see this as a problem?" I asked, responding to his affec-tive tone.

He was quiet for a few moments. "I don't know what the point is," he said. "I can't seem to finish anything."

"Why is that a problem?" I asked him. I found myself toying with the idea of "too much." Why should he have to stolidly fin-ish something rather than stopping when he was full? Why should he have to finish at all? Perhaps finishing was not the point but merely something that got in the way of finding it. "I have this image of a table laden with a banquet," I said, "and I'm wondering whether the person who must finish eating is enviable or the person who can sample freely and eat more of whatever has appeal?"

There was a long pause and then Thomas said that some years ago, he had stopped taking a radio with him when he runs. He likes it best when he gets into this "zone" where he can play with a problem or idea. "It was really good while I was at my last job, because there was always something to work over." As I was listening to him talk about this zone he enters, I found I was in my own zone, imaging a statue I might create, fingering it lovingly in my mind. The enjoyment was quite palpable. "You love to play with ideas," I suggested.

"Yeah," he said. In that moment, we were both able to be in touch with the pleasure one can find in being able to create something from within one's self. This experience became an important reference point for Thomas. He was able to think in terms of having what he needs inside rather than thinking of himself as internally deficient and missing something.

This sense of lack, of missing something, had left Thomas wondering whether he should be taking medication temporarily as a way of improving his functioning. He thought that medication might help him deal more effectively with the issues we were working on in the analysis, and then he would be able to get off the medication. The hazard in this view, however, was that it affirmed the idea that he was deficient and could not thrive on his own terms. I said that if his goal was ultimately not to take medication, it might be more worthwhile to better understand how he does function so that he can learn to work with the types of difficulties he was encountering.

It seems as though you have always been told that there is something wrong with you. You have been trying to not think about having deficits, while at the same time believing in them. This makes it difficult for you to work with the parts of yourself that have been problematic in whatever ways. Rather than working through the problem while keeping it in mind, you split it off, so that you wind up dealing with an ostensible problem, that in some sense you know is not "The Problem," but you can't be conscious of The Problem and so can't really work with it. This results in an endless series of unsolvable problems, because even good solutions don't solve The Problem because of the sleight of hand at work.

Part of Thomas's legacy from his mother and father is the notion that he does not have what he needs in order to survive. Neither parent seems to have had sufficient resiliency to have been able to set their children free from the shackles of their own reality. In the parental version of reality, the mother could never be held accountable. And so Thomas learned to externalize his distress and internalize blame, which left him always feeling responsible for whatever calamities seemed to be imminent. Because the events for which he felt responsible were never really in his hands, however, he was never able to atone sufficiently to make reparation.

As Thomas began to recognize the impossible cycle in which he had become mired, he learned to take his own needs and feelings more seriously and was also better able to value his own internal resources. Such a change may be seen as a shift from reading the symptom as a sign (a saturated element or symbolic equation) to being able to read the symptom as a symbol, with all the inherent complexity, subtlety, nuance, and layering implied by that term. This shift from symptom to symbol marked Thomas's growing capacity to use his creativity as a resource, rather than obscuring it under the various rubrics of distractibility or ADD.

6

Klein's Paranoid–Schizoid and Depressive Positions

KLEIN (1935, 1946, 1952) added an extremely useful conceptualization to the literature when she began to describe a primitive type
of splitting in which aspects of reality could disappear. This is
an important concept for us to have in mind in the moment that
we are sitting with a patient and something that seemed as
though it was known between us suddenly disappears quite completely from view. At these moments, we need to be able to find
a way to get our bearings, so that we can know what is unknowable for the patient in a way that does not assault them but rather
carries the meaning until such time as they might be able to re-
encounter it.

Klein (1935, 1946) calls this state of unknowing the *paranoid– schizoid position*, combining Fairbairn's (1952) depictions
of an isolated, schizoid position with her own views of a primitive, persecutory phase in development in which unintegrated
hostility isolates the individual and invites fears of retaliatory
attacks. Klein describes the paranoid–schizoid position as a state
of fragmentation in which "good" and "bad" get dichotomized
into separate realities. This is where you see splitting, as though
you could have one part of a whole without inevitably having
to take into account the rest.

This type of good versus bad dichotomization is an essential
way of organizing the world. It is fed by parental figures who

appear to have the lock on these distinctions and come to seem in charge of dispensing final judgments. Part of the task of growing up is to accept the existence of shades of grey and the inevitability of having to make our own judgments and of accepting that others will not necessarily agree. From the paranoid–schizoid position there is an ultimate judge in the form of a per-secuting externalized Other, whereas from the depressive posi-tion there are merely judgments, both internal and external, and the possibility of disagreement without destruction.

In the paranoid–schizoid position, we tend to be residing in the realm of feeling, and reality is configured primarily by sen-sory and affective elements. As affect intensifies, it can be diffi-cult to access our more rational faculties (see chapter 10). Being able to titrate—or "contain"—the affect can help us to move into a space from which we might think about whatever is hap-pening rather than merely reflexively reacting to it (see, e.g., Ogden, 1985).

In contrast to the paranoid–schizoid position, which is dom-inated by affect, Klein (1935) describes another position, which she calls *depressive*. From the depressive position, good and bad aspects can each be accepted and taken into account. The depres-sive position involves being able to renounce our hope that we might be able to sit on one side of the continuum without hav-ing to allow for the other: it requires the integration of both. So, from the depressive position, we get the type of distance from the intensity of the lived moment that facilitates rational thought but, in the process, we find ourselves distanced from some of the emotional realities of the experience as lived.

Experientially, Klein's depiction of the paranoid–schizoid posi-tion seems to be a way of trying to talk about these spaces we get into where our realities are highly constrained because of the intensity of the affect. It is kind of like being in a tight little space with the walls closing in, so that there do not seem to be many options or roads out, except perhaps to attack or withdraw.

So, for example, think about when you have a transference reaction to someone: For me, it tends to be facsimiles of my older sister, whose great passion was finding things to exclude me from so she could leave me feeling wanting. As we were talking one day as adults, I said something about having had a difficult time learning to keep my equilibrium in her presence. She completely surprised me by smiling and saying: "Well, of course: That was the point."

So, thanks to the grace and insight that are also part of this personage I call "Karen," I was given a bit of life-saving distance. Her willingness to see both sides helped me to more fully do so as well. From this position of enhanced perspective, I could better think about the qualities I find problematic, rather than becoming too overwhelmed by my affective response to think at all. It is in these moments of heightened reactivity that we most need to be able to "make it different." Otherwise, the intensity of the affect seems to confirm our worst fears, and we are retraumatized. I have come to call people who elicit this response from me "Karen" people, which indexes for me the important qualities I have found really difficult to tolerate. We all have our Karen people, who seem to represent the critical other against whom we mark our value.

This phenomenon results from a type of condensation that Matte-Blanco (1975) calls *symmetrization*. As affect intensifies, meanings condense, and it becomes more and more difficult to make distinctions within the seeming sameness. Like becomes same, and it's hard to discriminate the distinctions that might give us some anchoring points. So, for some time, when I found myself in the presence of "Karen" people, I couldn't really be with them without feeling diminished or at least in dire peril of attack. In those moments, you find yourself in one of those realities that is configured in black and white terms—us and them—good and bad—the kind of tightly knit reality that does not leave much room for thought, much less exploration.

Sitting with someone who is locked into a paranoid–schizoid reality poses particular challenges for us as therapists, in part because we are locked out of the relationship in fundamental ways. We find ourselves being used as a bit player in a drama of the other person's making. So, for example, we encounter a patient whose anxiety is such that he cannot find the connecting links between any of the fragments of his experience. From his perspective, the therapist becomes the persecuting object who withholds from him the key to resolving his dilemma.

"It all goes to bits," the patient says, when we try to talk to him. "I don't know what to tell you because I don't know which bit you want. You don't tell me and I don't know how to choose." We can watch his agitation build as we try to understand how these "bits" or fragments of thought might link together into meanings that have become impossible for him to recognize. However, our very understanding threatens his uneasy equilibrium and so he fights this impending understanding with whatever resources he has at hand. In the moment, the patient's conviction that these bits do not and cannot link together is a desperate defense against the possible meanings they might have in my mind. Keeping them separate lessens his anxiety but also leaves him unable to function in a world in which we must be able to link up the bits in order to find meaning and build relationships.

Here you can see how valiantly this man holds on to the bits—the fragments of his experience—as a way of marking their importance without giving away their meaning. Keeping them in bits is a buffer against potential intrusion and annihilation. The world has become too dangerous to allow himself to be known without first ensuring his safety, ascertaining whether I can safeguard the bits without intrusion.

In this instance, the bits have become things. They are not useful as symbols but rather merely mark their potential usefulness, if we could be able to think about them more freely. Greater fluidity of thought would entail a movement from the paranoid

–schizoid realm of saturated meanings, in which the symbol is experienced as a concrete entity and there is no room for play, into the depressive realm of potential meanings, in which the symbol can stand for the object, and we have more freedom to play with possibilities (Klein, 1930; Segal, 1957).

The realm of the paranoid–schizoid position is a difficult one to be thrust into clinically. In the moment, we might be cast in the role of critical father; persecuting sibling; withholding mother. We find ourselves trying to wriggle out of a one-dimensional role that doesn't quite fit, but there's enough truth to it to leave us wriggling even harder. It's like one of those Chinese finger traps where the harder you fight, the more stuck you get. All you can really do is try to relax and accept the role, meanwhile resurrecting yourself by reminding yourself that although you are this, you are also more. That makes it a bit easier to accept the role in which you've been cast without getting so caught by it.

In this process, you have moved from the paranoid–schizoid to the depressive position. This shift entails renouncing our wish to sit on the good side of the good/bad dichotomy, so that we can accept whatever realities intrude themselves into the moment as best we can. (You will notice that in this movement, we have also begun to contain what had seemed uncontainable.) This movement entails our ability to accept that the persecuting other is not solely other but rather also represents a part of ourselves as well. Whether we view this critical other as an externalized superego function or as an aspect of self projected outward, the result tends to be the same. The critical other becomes a persecutory object because of our very agreement with the judgments being purveyed.

The paranoid–schizoid and the depressive positions are not discontinuous but reciprocal and interactive. Klein first spoke of them in linear, developmental terms, as though one could somehow leave behind the discomfort of the paranoid–schizoid forever. That, I think, was a wishful fantasy. In reality, life is a continuing process of moving back and forth between the fragmentation (and affective acuity) of the paranoid–schizoid toward the integration and assimilation (but also the greater affective distance) of the depressive. By way of conceptualizing a potential resolution to this dichotomy, Grotstein (2000) describes a position he terms *transcendent*, in which we move beyond the tensions between the paranoid–schizoid and depressive into a more freely creative space. This position, however, is not an ultimate resolution to our dilemma. We are continually challenged to move beyond any particular resolution in order to assimilate and integrate new understandings. Change requires continuous work!

The interplay between the paranoid–schizoid and depressive positions can be very odd to encounter clinically. We can perhaps see it most vividly in individuals who have a great deal of ambivalence over knowing certain facts of existence. For example, in my work with Kate (see chapter 4), who appeared to have been sexually abused as a child, "facts" that appeared to be known between us at one moment could disappear quite radically the next. I would find myself alluding to something we had discussed together and would encounter an absolute lack of recognition. Initially, this gap was quite disconcerting. Over time, however, I began to understand that my task was to be able to carry these difficult facts for Kate during the moments when she was not able to be aware of them. At times, it was only through the relative obscurity of her dreams that Kate could mark whatever realities she needed to both know and not know. Then, when she felt a bit sturdier, we could once again know these realities together and continue our work more explicitly (see Charles, 2002c, for a fuller explication of this case).

Although we might have the wish to leave our difficulties behind once and for all, growth is never final. Even Grotstein's (2000) transcendent position brings in new tensions and challenges, inviting us to move beyond the fragmentation and acceptance of the paranoid– schizoid and depressive positions and more creatively meet the lived moment. Although this conception encourages a movement toward creative and generative activity, it also tends to perpetuate the hope that we might find an enduring point of safety at the expense of the more realistic goal of building our resources sufficiently that none of the spaces we encounter will seem quite so dire. Each reality brings its own challenges and gives way to the processes of fragmentation through which new meanings emerge. As we ride this roller coaster, we need some picture to hold on to—to ground us and give us means for communication—but we also need to be able to move beyond the known, to help us find our way through the complexities that life offers.

Ultimately, this work requires that we arm ourselves with whatever aids in this journey of reciprocal understanding of self and other, and that we be willing to turn our attention with interest (in spite of whatever reluctance or terror we also encounter) toward whatever obstacles lie in our path. We need to be willing to encounter the mystery (Coltart, 1992) and to act in accordance with our own best instincts, whether or not we can "understand" them or foresee their consequences in the moment (Symington, 1983). At times, the monster that seems to bar the path would seem to be none other than devalued aspects of self, denied. We then must tame the monster by making its acquaintance. Klein (1946) describes this process of keeping the monster at bay by locating it outside of the self as *projective identification*, which will be discussed in chapter 8 after first looking at Winnicott's (1971) ideas of *transitional space* and *the use of an object*.

7

Transitional Space and the Use of an Object

"UNLESS THE OBSCURITY CAN be circumvented," says Bion (1991), "it will remain unobserved" (p. ix). As we try to find our way through the impasses in which we get caught with our patients, it is important to be able to shed some light on the things that become fixed and entrenched and cannot be thought about. We need some way to be able to play with an idea, to move it around and think about it from different angles. If nothing else, this reminds us that the entrenched aspect has more to do with the feeling of it than with some objective necessity.

This idea of perspective was brought into the literature quite pointedly through Winnicott's ideas about the *transitional space* and the *use of an object*. The idea is that we need that third dimension—what Ogden (1994) calls *the analytic third*—in order to have sufficient perspective to be able to be creative and to play with an idea or with one another. You may notice that this is also the space of Klein's depressive position. Depressive is something of a misnomer in that this position does not have much to do with depression, aside from the renunciation that comes from recognizing that one is not the complete and total center of the universe. This change in perspective tends to be as much a cause for relief as for despair; it gives one a bit more room to move.

Winnicott's conceptualization of transitional space marks a progression from concrete "realities" to the realm of fantasy and ideas. He had observed that infants begin to use intermediary objects to represent the mother in her absence and that they also seemed to be able to use space in the same creative way. Given a good-enough "holding" environment, the baby was able to play with the ideas of mother present and mother absent as a means toward titrating the anxieties associated with dependency and separation.

In Winnicott's (1971) view, the infant needs to be able to "destroy" the mother—in the sense of being able to be actively aggressive in some fashion—and have the mother survive in order to begin to act freely as a separate subject. This space in which the mother could be destroyed and yet survive is the space in which creative activity or "play" can occur. This space also marks the transition between what Klein (1930) and Segal (1957) call the *symbolic equation* (in which no distinction is made between the symbol and the object it represents) and the symbol proper (which stands for the object but is not confused with it). The ability to actively use symbols marks a pivotal step in our journey toward attaining a greater level of autonomy within the nexus of the interpersonal world.

For Winnicott, the ability to "use" an object in this fashion helps us to integrate our destructiveness as well as our separateness. According to this formulation, in order to be able to interact with the other as a separate, thinking being we must be able to learn that the other can survive our own attempts at destruction. This is a crucial function that requires the ability to hold two separate truths in mind. We can only afford to venture into this dangerous territory if we can keep in mind some sense of sanctuary.

Sanctuary depends on our ability to achieve object constancy. We must be able to hold the other in mind and to ascertain that they continue to exist in our absence. Winnicott (1971) describes the sense of magical control that children experience in their early years. This sense of omnipotence is related to the ability to engage the other seemingly at will. Magical control, however, is an illusion that must ultimately fail, giving way to the ability to engage with the other and to achieve actual efficacy in relationships. Winnicott (1971) posits the achievement of *object usage* as a developmental milestone through which we discover that objects (and ideas) can change without being permanently destroyed, and that we can attain sufficient control to make our own lack of omnipotence tolerable. The ability to use an object in this sense enables us to more fully become the Subject, to become the author of our own imaginings.

The integration of separateness and resilience lends new dimensions and possibilities to the capacity for relating. For Winnicott (1971), the capacity for play develops into a capacity for shared playing as we learn to accommodate to the play of an other. It also develops into the ability to play with ideas. Each of these depends on our capacity for engagement, which, in turn, requires that we are sufficiently separate to be able to distinguish self from other. We need the freedom imposed by our assurance of the other's ongoing subjectivity in order to truly play freely. In Gadamer's (1988) words, in order "to truly experience the play, one must be drawn into it, to forget one's self in the moment and be in the play" (p. 102). Play is only possible to the extent that one is free to *be* in the moment (in chapter 13, we consider more explicitly how this capacity for play might be developed in the therapeutic environment).

Many individuals come to us with little capacity for play. The therapeutic environment then provides a space within which a forum for play can be created, a "playground" in which we can look at the obstructions because we have created "an intermediate region" (Freud, 1914, p. 154) in which we can be ourselves sufficiently to move toward transformation (Sanville, 1991). This forum is fundamentally predicated on the interrelated capacities to be separate and yet connected; to destroy and also build.

Winnicott (1971) posits as a precondition for this relative freedom the capacity to "survive attack," which in the context of the therapeutic relationship means to "not retaliate" (p. 91). This capacity is what makes us different from other people the patient has encountered. It is not that we do not recognize what is difficult or aversive about being with this person but rather that we can experience it and accept it without retaliating. What we *do* try to do with it is to understand it and to communicate these understandings in ways that are helpful rather than hurtful.

At times, being helpful may mean not interpreting in spite of our sense that we might understand something important. There are times, as Winnicott (1971) notes, when our interpretations merely affirm for the patient their own insufficiency, whereas, if we are willing to wait, the person might be able to encounter the same truth we had stumbled upon. At these times, Winnicott suggests, our interpretations preempt the patient's understanding, obstructing their ability to come to know in their own way without being instructed. Unnecessary interpretations, from this vantage point, may be seen as destructive to the individual's autonomy and creativity, similar to the parent who gives too much and does not leave sufficient room for the child to learn from his or her own experience.

It can be difficult to know how to encourage the capacity for playfulness in the people with whom we work. Without playfulness, the work can seem very flat and dead. This lack of vitality may be seen as a function of the person's fear of bringing him- or herself more fully into the room. When this is the case, our initial efforts must focus on creating a safe environment in which the work might take place.

There are times, however, when the question is not merely one of safety but also of having profoundly lost touch with (or never learned) the ability to play. This difficulty in being able to use the space was a major factor in my work with David, who had had a tantalizing mother and an extremely punitive and critical father. Each of these models for relationship was profoundly unsafe. Although his mother had provided him with an opportunity to play, participation in the play had resulted in a collusion that had left David with profound feelings of shame and regret. David's one safe outlet for play had become his writing, which he was able to utilize privately as a way to keep his creativity alive. By keeping his work hidden, however, he affirmed his lack of faith in its value and denied himself any opportunity for disconfirming this belief.

Eventually, David was able to show me some of his writings, which helped us to keep in mind the more creative aspects of himself that could not be brought more directly into the room at that time. Shame was such a salient part of David's sense of self that he often found it impossible even to talk in my presence. David and I used metaphors as a way of creating a communal, shared system of meanings. These metaphors provided a transitional space in which we were able to build a narrative sufficiently distant from David's fears regarding himself that we could explore with some freedom. This interim space reduced the painful self-consciousness and enabled him to explore important aspects of self and relationship without becoming quite so immobilized (see Charles, 2004, for a more extensive treatment of this case).

With many individuals, it is extremely difficult to negotiate a space in which creative work might occur. There are times when the pragmatics are such that words are experienced as actions or concrete entities that leave no room to consider them from alternative perspectives. We are no longer engaged at the level of symbolic meanings but rather have regressed to the level of the symbolic equation. When this occurs, it is often at the level of "the real" that we are offered an invitation into the work. At times this occurs through displacement, which allows us to explore a difficult topic *because* we are considering it at a remove from the person him- or herself. This distance enables us to consider important dilemmas that would not otherwise be accessible without evoking the terrible shame that self-consciousness would bring.

For example, Nina has deposited her profound rage and hostility into a character in a novel she is writing. Her husband hates this character, perhaps sensing that she is an enemy; that she looms larger in Nina's consciousness in proportion to the rage that looms beneath the surface. In contrast, I feel a certain fondness for "Fern," this lost child who, perhaps, must be "tamed" like the fox in Saint-Exupéry's (1943) story of *The Little Prince*. Fern finds her way into the consulting room when Nina's rage becomes too pressing in her relationships outside. In accepting Fern into the consulting room, we are also inviting Nina to accept her rage as a legitimate part of herself that we might be able to know and accept. In this way, she learns that she can be rageful and also be Nina: She need not split off the "bad" parts of self as a price of acceptance.

In grappling with the issue of the rage, we can come to understand that the rage is merely a marker for the ostensibly unknowable experiences that lie beneath. These issues emerge in another form of displacement: in Nina's dreams, where she can mark the events that cannot be consciously known and yet must not be forgotten. One of our most difficult tasks as therapists can be to track the multitudes of meanings and symbols that are brought into the room, to order them and organize them, and to have a sense of when to speak and when to be silent. At times, merely to have the unknowable present in the room is an achievement of great proportions. Putting the material forward in a displaced fashion can afford us the opportunity to explore difficult material without the terrible self-consciousness and intensification of affect that can effectively foreclose any real discussion.

Another way that impossible realities enter into the treatment is through enactments, as the ostensibly unknowable is played out more actively on the therapeutic stage (McDougall, 1985). One example of enactment is what Klein (1946) terms *projective identification*. In projective identification, problematic aspects of self are not recognized within the self but rather are located only in the other. In this way, they become visible without evoking undue distress. We consider projective identification in some detail in chapter 8, as it provides somewhat disconcerting and yet extremely valuable information for the therapist, if only she can keep her bearings.

8

Projective Identification

ONE OF THE OBSTACLES we encounter as psychodynamic therapists has to do with trying to understand some of the nonverbal cues being communicated within the space. This is an area that has been very intriguing to me. One conceptualization I've found to be particularly useful—again from Klein (1946) and then elaborated more fully by her followers (see, e.g., Grotstein, 1981; Joseph, 1997; Alvarez, 1999)— is *projective identification.* I've already alluded to projective identification in talking about the experiential end of the paranoid–schizoid state, where the fragmentation lends itself to good versus bad dichotomies and so to splitting.

Projective identification has been confused, particularly in the United States, with what Sandler (1976) calls *role responsiveness.* Ogden (1979) does this, for example, by including the pull on the recipient as part of the definition. Tying the concept of projective identification to its impact on the receiver gets us into problems conceptually (Garfinkle, 2003), so I would like to talk about these two aspects separately even though, from the perspective of the therapist, they tend to go together.

Projective identification was originally described as an unconscious phantasy[1] in which parts of the self are located in another

---

1. I am using the spelling "ph-" for unconscious phantasy and "f-" for conscious fantasy in accordance with the distinction articulated by Segal (1981).

person. This displacement is a useful thing to be able to do; it lets us be aware of problematic parts of ourselves with the relative safety of distance. The fact that it also involves a lie gets us into trouble, but that's another matter. If you think of projective identification in terms of the container/contained model, you can see that it is a useful conceptualization to have in mind for the therapist, who can otherwise find herself quite perplexed as bits of self get dislocated and relocated seemingly without regard for any rules of order or logic (note that here we are in the realm of unconscious logic, which has its own rules; its own logic; see chapter 10).

Klein enhanced Freud's (1914, 1921) conceptualizations of processes of projection and identification by highlighting the fundamental link between the two. Projective identification is most often thought of in terms of primitive splitting processes, in which the bad parts of self are projected outward and denied within the self. However, we also use projective identification in projecting good aspects of self onto others (Klein, 1946; Grotstein, 1981). Brunet and Casoni (2001) suggest that "the first process is associated primarily to the paranoid-schizoid position, and concerns anal sadistic fantasies, while the second process is related to the depressive position, and is associated with the projection of loving libidinal components" (p. 141). Brunet and Casoni help to alleviate some of the confusions that have arisen around the term by distinguishing between the intrusive, the communicative, and the empathic aspects of this complex process.

I think that the reason that projective identification has been seen as a two-person process is that we tend to know it through our countertransference reactions; we find ourselves suddenly the recipient of a thought or emotion that doesn't quite fit.

Let me give you an example. Quite often we find ourselves seemingly more invested in the treatment than is the person who came to see us because of a problem that was certainly his at the time. Suddenly, there he is, blasé as can be, with no idea of why we keep insisting that there is a problem—or that it might be worth tackling. In this instance, we can see that the patient's ambivalence has been split, so that the reluctance to enter treatment is located in the self, while the desire for it has been located in the therapist. We find ourselves the recipient of the patient's investment in the work that he is not able to own. The task then is to acknowledge and help the person work through the ambivalence, rather than acting it out as an opposition between patient and therapist.

Another forum in which projective identification enters the room is through disavowed, displaced affect. There are affects that tend to be difficult for people to own, and we may discover the importance of a particular affect when we notice it missing in the patient but present in ourselves! Anger is a big one; also sadness. We often find ourselves in the role of the keeper of the other person's disowned emotion. This displacement can be very useful. It provides an opportunity to have a conversation about the anger or the sadness that happens to be in the room, without the person getting so close to it that the feelings become overwhelming and cannot be thought about. Often, in the process of talking about it, we can detoxify it sufficiently (containment, once again) that the person can begin to take ownership of the feelings.

One of the ways we begin to become aware of projective identification in a given treatment is that we find ourselves preoccupied or distressed in a manner that takes us beyond our usual parameters. This process is easier to notice at a remove. For example, when I receive an urgent call from a supervisee who has become quite alarmed by a particular patient, I take the alarm seriously and we make sure that whatever safety measures might be important are in place, but then we also watch to see what occurs in the process. If the treatment is going well, what tends to occur is that the therapist becomes the recipient of the alarm that the patient had been feeling. The therapist then spends a very uncomfortable interval until the next session. At that time, he discovers that the patient is feeling markedly better.

What has happened, at another level, is that the patient has been able to deposit the distress, for safekeeping, in the therapist. As the therapist comes to understand the gravity of the situation, the patient is relieved of the burden of carrying the distress alone. Relieved, too, is the urgency of the need to have someone understand how pressing the problem actually is (recall the dilemma of Ruth in chapter 3). In this way, our willingness to take the other person's distress seriously—and to care so intensely about their well-being—creates a container in which the distress can be relieved. Our task then, is to understand the process sufficiently that we can take our charge seriously but also to distinguish the intensity of the affect from an actual state of emergency so that *we* can survive the encounter as well.

At times, I only come upon the fact that I am containing something important for a patient by chance. I find myself preoccupied by something and begin to wonder why this particular preoccupation has come forward at this particular time. It is often a dilemma I thought I had resolved long ago but find surfacing once again, seemingly out of the blue. At these times, if I cast my net broadly, I begin to recognize that the theme that is absorbing me comes not from my own life but from some important thread being worked on by a patient. In this way, I find that a less conscious part of myself continues to process the work long after I have closed the consulting room door and seemingly gone on about my life. This would seem to be the empathic aspect of our projective identifications. There is a comfort in knowing that an unconscious part of me can register a need and attune to it without having to explicitly focus on my work through all my waking hours. I think this is not so different from the parent who can move from a sound sleep to absolute alertness at the slightest movement of a child in distress. Our attunement extends far beyond our conscious understanding of it. We will discuss the nonverbal realms—and the uses we make of them—in greater detail in later chapters.

There are many times when patients cannot communicate to us directly about something that deeply troubles them but for which they have no conscious words or language. At these times, enactments may be the only means for bringing the dilemma to our awareness. This is not so different from what occurs in play therapy with children, where the distress that cannot be put into words is acted out within the play. Enactments are sometimes viewed as a sign of a problem occurring within the treatment. More often, however, they provide an important means for bringing to awareness unknown facts requiring further elucidation.

Many of our experiences have not been encoded into verbal memory and thus may not be accessible to conscious awareness. Stress interferes with our ability to encode memories; traumatic events, in particular, are often inaccessible. However, research shows that the same conditions that inhibit the conscious memory of traumatic events can amplify the unconscious memory of those same events (LeDoux, 1999). As a result, early experiences of deprivation or abuse are often communicated quite saliently, albeit nonverbally, in the transference.

As we take in these nonverbal communications affectively, we begin to have an experiential sense of the disembodied pieces of the patient's life without necessarily having sufficient verbal history to contextualize it. Over time, however, if we appreciate the value of these bits of experience, we can begin to put them together in a way that makes sufficient emotional sense that our newly found comfort begins to engender some relief in the patient as well. This relief in turn helps engender sufficient emotional distance from the alarm that we can begin to bring our thoughts to bear in a more productive way. At this point, we can also begin to think more explicitly about putting into words our ideas as to possible meanings of these previously disembodied fragments.

Consider for example the case of a woman who came to me after having spent many years trying to put together the facts of whatever had disrupted her development. Laurie had been sent to me by her previous therapist in the hope that we might be able to break through the impasse they had reached after 10 years of very intensive work. Many years of trying to recall the details of what seemed to be a history of sexual abuse had left Laurie with only fragments. There were no tangible memories of the suspected abuse from which to piece together the missing memories. The memories remained elusive, and the situation seemed to have become one in which she found herself persecuted by the missing memories.

Laurie's urgency seemed to result in part from her frustration, as she repeatedly flailed against a wall that seemed impenetrable. Soon I began to sense that we might be heading in the wrong direction, that this urgent focus on the past had become in many ways an avoidance of the present. I brought up the possibility that the elusive memories might prove to be beyond retrieval or, alternatively, that they might surface in their own time as she became better able to cope more generally. I suggested that it might be better to turn our focus from the past to the present. In this way, she could turn her energies away from what had been a very frustrating and unproductive search, toward building the life that was waiting to be lived.

Then, Laurie came in one night completely overwhelmed emotionally. She began to put forward disparate bits of experiences that had been evoked by her visit to a physician's office the previous day. She was so clearly on the edge that it seemed important to help her to pull these fragments together in a way that might help give her some grounding rather than merely asking her to tolerate this "dance" at the edge of the precipice. I felt on the edge, as well, as I really had nothing to offer beyond the observation that these pieces somehow came together into an experience of unremediated terror, with no help in sight. She seemed to be experiencing this terror, in the moment, as a fear of being pulled into an unredeemable and irretrievable "craziness."

In this moment, Laurie's terror was a palpable reality in the room. She could not speak of it in words but only through the language of affect as it played through her body and across her face. This was a moment when it seemed crucial that I accept the terror and take it in as my own as a way of perhaps helping Laurie (and myself) to find her way through it. In the moment, I spoke from my own experience of imagining myself inside the terrifying universe in which Laurie appeared to be caught. I spoke as a way of trying to titrate the terror and thereby to extricate us both without losing whatever might be gained from having shared this moment.

I tried to detoxify the fear by invoking thinking and putting my thoughts into words. I offered what I had, which was a belief that Laurie could survive—that things need not be as dire as they seemed. I told Laurie that I did not believe that she was going crazy but rather that she was in touch with a memory of having been in a completely impossible space with no relief in sight. This interpretation did indeed relieve her distress sufficiently that she was able to begin to imagine being able to think about how some of these pieces might fit together without feeling as though such activity would lead to immediate annihilation.

The unattainable memory had come to hold Laurie's hopes for salvation. Paradoxically, by moving out of the desperate, interlocked paranoid–schizoid space in which she was locked, Laurie was able to move into the very space from which she had felt barred. Her willingness to accept whatever might be possible had helped her to be more present with her actual feelings in the moment. This perspective enabled her to encounter the feelings of the past sufficiently to be able to make them present in a way that enabled us to begin to make sense of them. The new grounding helped us to piece together a few more fragments of her story in a way that was useful rather than feeling overwhelming and persecutory, as though she must then "go crazy" in defense.

You can see in this interaction a move from the paranoid–schizoid reality (in which her fear of going crazy meant that she was in imminent danger of doing so) to the depressive realm (in which her fear of going crazy could be understood as a fear rather than an imminent fact). This movement entails being able to separate or, in Matte-Blanco's (1975) terms, to *de-symmetrize* experiences that feel the same at a certain level of intensity and yet may be different in important ways (we discuss this further in chapter 10).

The movement from the paranoid–schizoid to the depressive position can be viewed as a move from a two-dimensional space in which realities seem fixed and immutable, to a three-dimensional reality in which we have the added third perspective from which to consider that reality and more actively think about it. As noted earlier, in the two-dimensional reality, we are in the domain of what Klein (1930) and Segal (1957) call the *symbolic equation*, in which the symbol cannot be separated from its manifestation. In this way, it is not useful as a symbol. This third perspective brings us into the realm of what Winnicott calls the *transitional space* (see chapter 7). It affords us a bit more room to play with ideas rather than being persecuted by ostensibly indigestible "facts." With the advent of perspective, we have the freedom with which to reflect on a symbol and to consider its various aspects and possible meanings. It no longer persecutes us with The Meaning that assaults us in the paranoid–schizoid reality.

Projective identification has that immediacy. In the moment, we are caught in whatever reality is being experienced by the other. It is palpable. In this way, it clearly has its interpersonal aspects as a lived experience. Perhaps the most important issue in reminding ourselves that projective identification is an *intrapersonal* event is to be able to keep straight in our own minds the unconscious nature of the communication. This perspective can help to titrate our own urge to "give it back" without first digesting it. If we can tolerate the feelings enough to be able to hold on to them and think about them, we might be able to make use of them in such a way that they can be taken in by the other, rather than passing them back and forth like a game of hot potato. As we come up against these pushes and pulls within ourselves and within the relationship, it is often very useful to be able to move beyond the ostensible meaning of an act or statement and to think about the intent. This challenge brings us into the realm of truth and lie, which we explore in chapter 9.

9

Truth and Lies

LET ME SEGUE A BIT HERE and talk about this idea of the *lie*, which is a very important concept to have in mind as we pursue our goals.

The lie tends to be a very slippery concept, highly dependent on our acuity, our perceptiveness, and our integrity. My views on truth and lies have been framed through the work of Wilfred Bion (1977), who is responsible for the title of this book and also for the fact that I'm writing it at all, because the adage "learning from experience" became a kind of mantra for me as I took deep breaths and tried, in spite of my terror, to trust what seemed to me to be true.

This terror was a function of the tension between my ideas regarding how therapy is "supposed to be" and my own sensibilities in the moment. As we've discussed previously, although theory helps us to anchor and organize our perceptions, it can also become a screen obstructing our view. If we are willing to face difficult truths, our intuitions of the moment can be our best guide in discriminating what is false from what is true.

In giving primacy to the individual's experience in the moment, Bion brings us up against this crucial and elusive question: How do we steer toward truth and avoid the lie? Most particularly, how do we confront those little lies we tell ourselves in our attempts to ease our discomfort at one turn or another?

Let me give you a clinical illustration to help convey a sense of my meaning. First, however, let us note that Bion's thoughts about truth, lie, and falsity are based on his explorations of distinctions between appearance and function. The idea here is that the same statement can be used for multiple purposes. The crucial issue, for Bion, is whether we are moving in the direction of evasion or growth. This may be quite difficult to determine, as we are inevitably caught by our ambivalence; the part of us that would like to know more versus the part that is afraid of what we might encounter beneath the veil.

The idea of the lie was highlighted in my work with David. David had had an abusive and intrusive father, which made self-protection more important than self-understanding. In our work together, it often feels to me as though we are in the midst of a treacherous sea of slippery waves that alternately reveal and obscure whatever "truths" we are seeking and avoiding. At times, David finds it tremendously difficult even to hold on to the sense of whatever he might be saying. He will say: "I don't know," and *I* won't know whether that statement was true in the moment, as the awareness began to disappear, or whether it had been a lie that had then made the statement *become* true. The question hinges on how much volition there had been in the moment, as the meaning disappeared.

So then, we come to this issue of lie versus falsity. To make this distinction, we need to know whether the person knows that they are speaking falsely or merely doing so without awareness. Bion puts it this way:

> It became evident that a distinction would need to be made between a lying statement and a false statement, the false statement being related more to the inadequacy of the human being . . . who cannot feel confident in his ability to be aware of the "truth," [versus] the liar who has to be certain of his knowledge of the truth in order to be sure not to blunder into it by accident [Bion, 1980, p. 5].

So, in order to lie, one needs to be sufficiently aware of the truth to consciously avoid it. Falsity, on the other hand, is a function of not knowing the truth, an inherent aspect of our human dilemma.

With David, I wonder (quite actively at times) whether we are in the realm of false statements or lies and how we might distinguish between the two. This would seem to be an essential dilemma for David. How can he know aspects of himself that he finds so distasteful that they have become virtually unknowable, especially in the face of his determined efforts over the years to divorce himself from the self that he would rather not know?

One day we found ourselves faced with this dilemma of the lie. He had said "I don't know," and I asked him whether this was a statement of fact or a statement he was hoping to make fact in the moment, or a lie that he was hoping would end the subject. David clearly felt put on the spot and so I tried to help him to see the point of my question rather than merely experiencing it as an attack. The question seemed important, I said, because it had to do with whether or not *he* knew what was true, which was much more important than whatever he might or might not tell me.

"I'm not sure," said David, "but it reminds me that I did tell a lie this morning, a really stupid lie. I don't know why I did that." I asked him to tell me more, and he recounted to me a story of having lied to a salesperson about a really trivial piece of information—the spelling of the name of his street. I asked him how he had felt at the time. "Anxious," he replied.

As David spoke, I had the sense that there had been some enjoyment for him in this interchange and therefore suggested that what he had experienced as anxiety could also be seen as exhilaration. It seemed as though he had been enjoying the lie because it left him knowing something the other person had not. The greater knowledge made him feel superior, rather than inferior and therefore vulnerable.

David did not agree with this idea of exhilaration, but as we moved on and he continued to affirm the triviality and meaninglessness of the lie, I wondered aloud about the hostility that seemed to accompany the lie. At first he denied it (he was not aware of it), but then as I began to talk about my ideas of the situation—how he seemed to have a somewhat disparaging attitude toward this person who could not spell and had then proceeded to actively encourage the misspelling—David began to be able to acknowledge the hostility inherent in the situation. At this point, the idea of the exhilaration could also be explored: There *had* been some enjoyment in the hostility, for which he had felt guilt and also some fear of discovery. His only awareness in the moment, however, had been of anxiety.

"This gives us an important piece of information," I said. "Now we know that it is easier for you to be aware of your anxiety than of your hostility in some moments when both are present. At times, then, the anxiety will be a cue alerting us to the presence of hostility."

This interchange highlights the usefulness of being aware of subtleties—such as the difference between the lie and the lack of awareness—that help us to make sense of what is going on within the process, even when the individual is not able (ostensibly) to bring forward the material that troubles him. The material is there—in another form, at another level. It is there metaphorically, so that part of the dance is to be able to discover what might be known and when, and the parameters within which meanings can be established.

With David, for example, we have had to agree on basic facts, such as the meanings of statements such as "I don't know." In this way, we are also having a discussion about the process of analysis and our preconceptions, which do not always agree. From his side, it seems to be a place in which help might be found but only theoretically. This keeps him able to persevere in coming to sessions, even though they are often frustrating and ostensibly unproductive. From my side, I tell David my beliefs about what might be possible in this space we are creating and also what possibilities seem to exist for him in the difficult moments in which little feels possible. In this way, his speechlessness is not merely an impediment to the process but also a meaningful act that we can attempt to understand in the moment (see Charles, 2002b).

This small piece of my work with David highlights the problem of the lie but, as with most things, also obscures it by enticing us to see the lie as Other—as alien. The lie, however, is really a constant companion—an ever-present danger—in terms of our desires to distort, distend, and discount certain aspects of reality that seem awkward, unpleasant, or humiliating. As we try to avoid these truths, we also avoid opportunities to understand them better and to begin to work them through until we arrive at another hard edge we are not quite ready to penetrate.

We are not only up against the other person's lies/limits: We are also up against our own. The unconscious being what it is, we often don't really know our limits until we find ourselves right up against them. This makes it crucial that we try as best we can to be open to whatever we happen to be experiencing in the moment and to try to think about it—to consider the range of possible meanings.

Here is an example from my own experience. I gave up caffeine many years ago in the interests of trying to find a better grounding in myself, a greater equilibrium. I wanted some peace, and giving up caffeine was a part of that determination and came to have other meanings for me as well, some positive and some not so positive, such as a certain elitism I felt in "not indulging." In this fashion, meanings build upon meanings and come to imprison us in their various ways. After much time had passed and this noncaffeine self had become entrenched, I found myself in France, where caffeine is not the disparaged evil it has come to be among the health-conscious in this country. Like a kid in a candy store, I found myself confronted with this new kick. It was interesting to encounter caffeine once again, but this time with much fuller cognizance of the drug it really is.

Segue, now, to my son's injury, which occurred hard on the heels of my trip to France, thrusting me precipitously into a new reality in which peace was hard to come by and sleep along with it. I sat in my therapist's chair through those long months of not-peak form, knowing that there is a benefit to being thrust headlong into the harsh realities of life, in that it enables us to sit with our patients' pain so much more profoundly without running and hiding from *that* particular peril.

But then, there was this *other* side: I was tired and not well able to find my bearing when encountering the type of long-winded evasion that has always engendered a marked sleepiness in me. At times, fending off the drooping eyelids becomes such a full-time task, and seems so concrete an evidence of my own incapacities, that I lose any sense of perspective or ability to be interested in other potential meanings. This battle at times requires so much of my energies that I am firmly taken aback when confronted.

"You know, it's really hard to talk to someone who's falling asleep," says Elena. "I'd like to go get you a cup of coffee or something."

The first time this happens, I am too overcome by embarrassment and regret to do much with it, other than just try to survive the moment. It's difficult to get my bearings within the analytic space, because the pragmatics of the situation seem so pressing. I am so aware of the "real" reasons for my tiredness that I am not able to consider other possible meanings that might help us understand why my tiredness has become such an issue at this moment, in this session.

Blindly determined not to be caught once again, I begin to add a cup of espresso to my midday meal, which comes right before Elena's sessions. This routine seems to work quite well on the whole, until one day I find myself mildly bored and distracted and tired, and Elena confronts me again. Inwardly, I squirm, and there is guilt and alarm and regret and all of that, but alongside, there is also the awareness that I am not all that tired, and that even when I am, I can be called to attention at a moment's notice by the appearance in the room of something that feels real and compelling.

So I begin to speak to Elena through whatever embarrassment or shame might also be attendant. I speak to her of this facet of our interaction that seems as though it might be worth understanding: What is it about our process that results in this type of occurrence? I offer my reflections on it—that she seemed to be actively not feeling anything about something that was very important. And that perhaps, just as I resonate to her pain and her pleasure, I also resonate to her lack of feeling. This idea helped us to be able to focus on what was missing in the room and in Elena; her feelings about the things that are most precious to her and seem most terrifying and most out of reach.

On occasion, Elena had told me that she finds it difficult even to think about the things that most trouble her because they disappear. She described how, in the moment, her focus switches and she's off to something else, without even remembering what had come before. The problem is that what most troubles her does not bother her at all because she does not think about it. And that's the real problem: that she might lose sight of it forever and never get it back; that she might continue to live this quite happy—but at some level intolerably empty—life without ever getting back the things that make life meaningful.

As I regain my bearings and focus once again on Elena and her experience, my own terrible experience of failing to hold onto the moment—of failing to hold on to Elena—recedes sufficiently that I can appreciate how fundamentally it conforms to what Elena has been trying to communicate to me. Although her words had failed to communicate the magnitude of her experience, in the transference we had provided an opportunity for greater understanding by creating an experience that was configured along the lines of Elena's own experience of losing herself. In this way, my willingness to be lost was an absolute prerequisite for being able to find ourselves more fully and more profoundly.

This is the type of interaction that Levenson (1988) so eloquently describes, in which it is the "isomorphic recreation of the content of her fantasy, occurring as she tells it" (p. 11) that vivifies the material. For Levenson, "it is this remarkably recursive, mirror-image quality of [the] interaction, which, in my view, gives transference its power, its ability to create a 'show and tell' playground" (p. 11).

Because of this intensification, in the consulting room we find ourselves sitting with realities that often truly are too intolerable to bear; realities that from the outside might not seem so terrible, but, in the moment, oh, in the moment they can seem impossible. Tolerating our annoyance, our irritation, our boredom, our stupidity, our clumsiness, our hatred—whatever it might be that seems difficult or impossible to know in the moment—these are the real challenges in our work. They push us to fine-tune our conceptualizations to aid both our survival and our efficacy, a subject we turn to in the next chapter.

10

Patterns

IN THIS PROCESS OF trying to become more fully myself as a clinician and as a person, there have been certain things that have intrigued me that have become the grist for my writings. My theory tends to be drawn out of the difficulties I experience in the work. It represents the current status of my attempts to work my way through these enigmas.

My ideas about *patterns*, for example, grew out of an emerging sense that there were meanings being communicated back and forth in ways that went beyond the verbal interchange (Charles, 2002a). The ability to access and communicate these nonverbal meanings seems to be important not only to our work but also to creative activity more generally. Theorists have linked the capacity for creative thought and action to parts of the mind that function by pattern recognition (see, e.g., Ehrenzweig, 1967; Trevarthen, 1995). Many creative breakthroughs, such as the benzene ring for example, have been first intuited from the form of the pattern. Einstein once said that he rarely thought in words at all but rather that his ideas often came to him fully formed, at which point he would try to find words to express them (Opatow, 1997).

There seems to be an optimal balance between the ability to register these types of patterned, nonverbal meanings and the ability to think about our experiences more explicitly. Overwhelming affect, such as that associated with trauma, tends to inhibit the very types of cognitive functions that enable us to process and make sense of our experience. Matte-Blanco's (1975, 1988) analyses brought into the literature some very useful ways of conceptualizing patterns of thinking as well as the complex interrelationships between thoughts and feelings. His conceptualizations help us to understand both creativity and that other extreme—the affective and thought deficits associated with the sequelae of extreme trauma.

Freud (1915) noted certain rules and regularities associated with primary process (less conscious; more highly driven by affect) thinking versus those that inhere in secondary process (more conscious; rational) thinking. Using mathematical set theory, Matte-Blanco (1975) helps to pinpoint some of those essential distinctions by framing them in terms of the "symmetrical" logic that dominates unconscious thinking and the "asymmetrical" logic that dominates conscious thought.

In order to do this, Matte-Blanco builds on the mathematical notion of "infinite sets." This theory suggests that as sets become larger, the gradations that distinguish one member from another disappear. This is the domain of unconscious logic, which is quite distinct from the more conventional, asymmetrical logic that dominates conscious thought. Asymmetry is the domain of distinctions. In asymmetrical logic, there are specified relationships that are not necessarily reversible. For example, A is the father of B does *not* mean that B is the father of A.

In contrast, symmetrical logic dominates the unconscious, in which the conditions noted by Freud (1915), such as displacement, condensation, timelessness, the absence of mutual contradiction and negation, and the replacement of external by internal reality, "sometimes designated as literal interpretation of metaphor" (Matte-Blanco, 1959, p. 2), rule. This is the domain of similarity among seemingly unlike things, in which the part becomes the whole, time and space disappear, "like" becomes "same," and valenced relationships seem reciprocal.

Noting the logic of the unconscious helps us to understand its rules and regularities, so that we might begin to discern meanings in what, at first glance, seems to be meaningless. All thought contains some mixture of symmetrical and asymmetrical thought. One of the very interesting things that Matte-Blanco (1975) notes, however, is that as affect intensifies, symmetrical thought tends to predominate. This results in overinclusive classes, in which meanings are condensed and distinguishing features tend to be lost. This makes it increasingly difficult to distinguish differences between similar objects or to specify relationships between the objects.

With unconscious, symmetrical logic, we lose the type of grounding that comes from our ability to make distinctions by naming and categorizing. Matte-Blanco's observation that affect symmetrizes experience has been affirmed by memory studies: Intense affective experiences seem to be stored in such a way that any facet that has been linked to the experience can evoke a resurgence of the affect (Bucci, 1997). Trauma not only impedes affective self-regulation but also results in the type of unlinking of thoughts associated with the paranoid–schizoid position more normatively or in psychotic disorders at the further extreme. It also results in the type of unlinking of ideational memory and affect that we see in many patients.

This lack of linking between affect and ideation can be quite profound. It can be difficult even to imagine the extent of the disjunction until we encounter it clinically. For example, I worked with one man who had begun abusing substances in his teens as a way of distancing himself from intolerable feelings. Denial and substance use became his only means for titrating strong emotions. These defenses effectively precluded his development through his adolescent years. As he neared adulthood, Craig obtained treatment for the substance abuse and settled into a somewhat more adaptive pattern in which he was able to function at work and at home while maintaining his emotional equilibrium through binge drinking. At the point at which he finally sought treatment from me, the consequences of the alcohol abuse had become intolerable. Without alcohol, however, he had no way of even acknowledging his emotions, much less learning to tolerate them. This deficit had resulted in two serious suicide gestures that quite remarkably seemed to have passed by the hospital censors without raising due alarm.

My alarm became a reference point by which we could begin to mark the magnitude of his distress. As we tried to understand the feelings that Craig had no awareness of, we were often out of synch with one another. His lack of conscious awareness kept me off balance, as his placid exterior belied the turmoil that seemed to lurk just below the surface. It was as though my perceptions had no grounding in consensual awareness, even though they continued to be affirmed by the ongoing chaos he was creating in his life.

As a way of trying to create a shared reality, I began to recount to Craig some of the signs of distress I was seeing. I described the flooding of affect in his face when we hit on a distressing subject, which then was replaced quite remarkably by apparent calm as he began to think about the possible causes of his distress. In the transition, his distress became as remote and inaccessible for him as the childhood experiences I wondered about, but which Craig could not easily recall. His initial response was to assume that nothing was there, and it took a great deal of exploring and conjecture on my part to create an opening through which Craig might begin to focus sufficiently on the past or on feelings to be able to begin to encounter them.

In the meantime, being able to share the image of the affective flooding and its sudden disappearance helped us to mark a *shared focus of inquiry*. In this way, we began to piece together a story that would make sense of Craig's experience as he recounted it, assembled from the brief moments when affect was not entirely annihilated by thought. It was an odd journey for both of us, as we translated his world into a dialect that took into account the child who had yearned for his mother's affection and whose emotional reality had been perpetually denied and overridden.

Matte-Blanco's ideas of symmetry and asymmetry offer an interesting way of understanding this dialectical process of integrating thought and feeling, which is also useful to us in understanding the process of transference. We can conceptualize *transference* as an intrusion of past into present without being able to mark important distinctions. For example, the more reactive I am to the qualities I found aversive in my older sister, the less able I am to distinguish between people who may be like, yet unlike, her. In this way, my danger signals may be firing wildly in the presence of someone whose only threat might be a casual or superficial resemblance that bears little or no relation to the toxic qualities I am trying to keep at bay.

Similarly, as Craig splits off awareness of his affect and I become the only person in the room who registers that affect, I also become the deprecating authority figure from whom he must hide. The nightmare from which Craig hides—but continually plays out in his interpersonal world—seems to be patterned after his relationship with his mother, whom he longed to please but could not. For Craig, it is iterations of his mother that are most threatening to his fragile self-esteem. The further he moves from the position of the "good boy," the greater is his need to hide from being seen as the "bad boy." Either position precludes development toward taking a stand as an autonomous adult. In some ways, Craig's addiction to alcohol may be seen as a way of hiding from his mother while also defying her. His inability to consciously choose to defy the feared other, however, affirms his negative self-attributions and self-deprecation and thereby also confirms the perceived need to hide, which in turn perpetuates the alcohol use.

In these scenarios, we can see the type of condensation or symmetrization in which classes of items become equivalent. In the moment, the experienced similarity to the feared other impedes the type of rational thought necessary to make needed distinctions. This type of intrusion of past into present is particularly problematic with fear reactions, which become entrenched easily and are remarkably difficult to unlearn because the survival value of fear "imprinting" tends to outweigh the need to overrule irrational fears (LeDoux, 2002). Principles of asymmetry also come into play here: I may be impeded in acknowledging and building within myself qualities that may be important to my development but have too firmly become "other" by virtue of their alignment with the "other side" (Charles, 2001a).

Avoidant defenses further amplify the dilemma by precluding new learning. Adaptation depends on our ability to use both symmetry (noting similarities) and asymmetry (being able to distinguish differences) toward greater understanding. Crucial to this is our ability to be sufficiently present in our own experience to encounter patterns of equivalencies and disjunctions and to be able to make sense of them in meaningful ways.

Depending on where we begin, for the therapist, this might entail heightening the distress we encounter or diminishing it, depending on our sense of what is feeding the obscurity. Bion (1970, 1991), following Freud, speaks of "deepening the darkness" as a way of enabling ourselves to make out the faint illuminations within it. We must continually negotiate between our evasive and adaptive urges, which are often intertwined too tightly to allow much respite from this task.

When we are caught in the mire of paranoid–schizoid realities, Matte-Blanco's lexicon offers a useful way out. Noting differences within a seeming sameness helps us to ground ourselves when forced disjunctions have become the rule. For example, some people's vocabularies are so densely symmetrized that we only come to realize this fact as we find ourselves trying to extricate ourselves from the mess. At times we might find ourselves avoiding particular areas of inquiry lest we be cast as the villain once again. At other times we wind up tying ourselves in knots to avoid the feared attack or retreat as the person encounters the reviled quality in us that so immediately toxifies the whole.

Until we can see the pattern being played out, we have little idea of where we are caught or how to find our bearings. It is only when the pattern has been illuminated that we can begin to imagine a way of stepping outside of it and casting some light into the darkness—or darkness into the light. It is often by our uneasy sense of an unnamed and uncomfortable consensus that we begin to discover the implicit pacts we have made. For example, I worked with a woman who had a terrible time leaving at the end of her sessions. She would find one way or another to stretch out the last few minutes, often by saying so little during the hour that her increased animation at the end was a welcome relief and also seemed too important to disturb.

My acceptance of these conditions, however, seemed also to be in secret collaboration with a part of herself that only seemed to be able to value the part of the hour for which she was not paying. My attempt to confront this issue was experienced by her as an explosion that fairly blasted her out of the room and was so distressing that we reeled from it for some time. Yet, it was important for her to be able to speak to the importance of those unpaid moments—through which she took some false assurance of care—in order for us to be able to move further into a whole complex of issues regarding her place in a universe in which vital supplies belong only to the other and not to the self, and in which one is continually at the mercy of those who control the supplies. Deconstructing the layers of these assumptions has been an ongoing and extremely enlightening process.

Our ability to integrate nonverbal aspects of communication is essential for any real understanding. This is particularly important in the consulting room, in which we are charged with receiving communications that have not yet been consciously formulated by the other person. La Barre (2001), for example, noted the complex "choreographies of conversation" (p. 2) that guide and inform our interactions. As therapists, we must be able to resonate to the subtleties and nuance that patients bring into the room, in order to begin to have a sense of what their world is like and where they get stuck (we will look at this resonance in more detail in chapters 12 and 13). Often, we find ourselves immersed in an enactment that carries the pattern of that person's interpersonal engagements. In being able to participate with the person in these engagements, we have a much better sense of some of the complexities involved. However, we also have a sense of discomfort in feeling as though our selfhood has been usurped and our more rational capacities overwhelmed.

As the discomfort increases, the affect intensifies. Any event that is highly saturated in affect tends to work against asymmetrical—or conventionally logical—thought. "Extreme emotional states display qualities of irradiation, maximalization and time and space tend to disappear . . . at its height grief irradiates, everything good is felt as lost for all eternity" (Rayner, 1981, p. 409). Conversely, the denial of affect precludes any real engagement with others. Our task is to develop our ability to be able to feel an experience and also think about it. We need to be able to make room for both the rational and nonverbal elements in order to come to an empathic understanding in which neither self nor other is lost.

At moments of intense affective engagement, if we are willing to continue to interact while also continuing to wonder about what is taking place, we can retain sufficient balance between the affective and cognitive pieces to enable us eventually to find our way. At times, however, we find ourselves immersed and having to think later, whereas at other times we will find that we have short-circuited the process because of our discomfort. Although we would like to be able to keep our equilibrium in the moment, this balance is often only achieved over time as we process the complexities of the work within ourselves.

One of our tasks in this work is to come to know, and to make known in verbal form, experiences that are communicated via other domains. As therapists, we align ourselves with the patterns of our patients' ways of being in the world. Our empathic attunement becomes a key to understanding the other person's world. Our attempts at attunement also provide a model that helps the other person to become more attuned to him- or herself. In this way, we help the individual to incorporate rhythms of safety and soothing (Tustin, 1986) to replace (or at least to supplement) the rhythms of startle, discord, and disconnection that otherwise prevail. Through these reciprocal interactions, meanings are made within the therapeutic dyad (Ogden, 1994). Our ability to make meanings together provides not only an avenue of greater understanding but also a source of hope.

Hope can be subverted in subtle ways as we come to accept the other person's visions of self in ways that serve to undermine their development. This dilemma can be particularly problematic with individuals who have little assurance of their own resiliency and capacity for survival and find it difficult to situate themselves as subject without invoking fears of attack or abandonment. At those times, it is important to get a sense of the patterns being played out so that we can begin to grasp the underlying issues.

For example, the bulimic repeatedly plays out her ambivalence over needing the other by first abstaining, in the wish that she might have no needs. Needs, however, eventually become pressing and the urgency to fill the void results in compulsive taking-in to the point of saturation and discomfort. This discomfort results in repugnance toward that which was taken in, causing the cycle to repeat itself. This type of dynamic emerges in interpersonal relationships as well, as the individual attempts to not need the other and then acts out the need (and the frustration) in other arenas.

Ryan, for example, played out this pattern with her therapist repeatedly. The therapist would encounter a "rule" that Ryan had set—such as not being able to call the therapist between sessions—through hearing how intolerable the interval had been for Ryan. It was easier for Ryan to become actively suicidal as an expression of her need and frustration than to ask for help more directly. This left the therapist feeling as though she should somehow magically know and be in charge of the distress that Ryan was unable to communicate. Understanding her own countertransference reactions helped the therapist to be aware of Ryan's wish along with the underlying feelings of helplessness, frustration, and anger that were also present. Her recognition of the implicit demands, and the potential price of meeting these, helped the therapist to focus more explicitly on Ryan's inability to make (or meet) demands. Rather than trying to "fix" the problem, they were able to process and better understand the patterns in play, to explore Ryan's intense neediness, rage, and fears of engulfing and overwhelming (and losing) the other.

This movement from the paranoid–schizoid position of symbolic equations (in which desire is experienced as desperate irresolvable need, and being saved by an other equals being loved) to the depressive position (in which one can consider how desires might be satisfied, and saving one's self is not tantamount to utter abandonment by the other) was a crucial one. In refraining from attempting to solve the problem, the therapist was implicitly disconfirming Ryan's view of herself as helpless and hopeless. Inviting Ryan to explore her dilemma and to think of possible resolutions was an essential step toward helping Ryan to believe that she could attend to her own needs without losing the other. This is one example of how closely interpersonal and developmental dilemmas can be configured to the pattern of the symptoms. In this way, the symptoms provide important clues as to how the person's interpersonal world is configured.

This is also a good example of how seemingly irrational behaviors can actually offer us important information about the dilemmas the individual is facing. Matte-Blanco's (1975, 1988) work helps to elucidate this whole process of meaning-making, by pointing to the reason that underlies what we often term the *irrational*. That term is often a euphemism for whatever is yet unknown and so seems incomprehensible. Although we have many ways of knowing that have little to do with rational, verbal thought, we tend to underestimate the importance of attending to sensory information from other modalities. However, these *primitive communications*, as McDougall (1980) calls them, are a potent source of information if we can learn to attune ourselves to the right key or channel. Many authors have pointed to the wealth of information that may be passed from one person to another without being elucidated in verbal form. Balint (1953) affirmed the importance of enriching our understanding through the inclusion of other spheres, such as rhythmicity, a very basic form of pattern. More recent authors, such as Knoblauch (2000) and La Barre (2001), have heightened our appreciation of the diversity and complexity of the processes by which we discern meanings from formal aspects of interchange, thereby also enhancing our understanding of some of the subtleties and intricacies of these highly patterned nonverbal elements.

Nonverbal communications are a special challenge in that we do not have the comfort of the word to reassure us that we are in the right place at the right time. We seem to be more comfortable in the register of the rational than in trusting our bodies as primary receptor organs. Most of us have been told too often, particularly as children but also as adults, that we did not really see what we thought we saw; hear what we heard; feel what we felt. This leads to a dual track of reality. We have an inner conviction that tends to be hidden as a way of safeguarding it.

This contrasts with an outer conviction that is more public, mediated by our perceptions of consensual reality. Our training can help us to tolerate the ambiguity but can also impede our ability to comprehend. As Meltzer (1975) notes, "We have from our education and development a massive preconception of models and theories and ideas that we gradually have to get rid of in order to free ourselves to receive new impressions and to think new thoughts and entertain new models" (p. 289). Meltzer's point is well exemplified in McCleary's (1992) candid description of her own evolution as a therapist, as the encounters with her patient forced her to challenge whatever theoretical constructs obstructed growth and understanding.

Any model can provide an opportunity to enlarge and enhance our understanding or can become a straightjacket that keeps us from thinking new thoughts or from seeing "outside of the box." Matte-Blanco's (1975, 1988) theory of bi-logic invites us to look at the formal structure underpinning Freud's theories of conscious and unconscious processes in ways that potentially enlarge our understanding. His work joins Bion's (1977) invitation to move beyond the content and look more carefully at the processes at work within our selves and within the therapeutic hour. This helps us to piece out, in Matte-Blanco's terms, the continuing interplay between the symmetrical and asymmetrical domains of being. It also helps us to keep in mind, in Bion's (1977) terms, whether we are moving in the direction of evasion or understanding.

11

Patterns as Templates
Understanding Transference

ONE OF THE MOST IMPORTANT cornerstones of our work is the idea of *transference*. Transference involves the unconscious application of previous patterns onto a current situation. This process is an adaptive one. We use our previous experience as a template from which to make sense of current interactions. It is when the pattern has been misapplied or does not fit that we notice the disjunction and call it transference.

This type of matching to pattern is the basis for how we learn. It also reflects the process of learning itself, in which *"remembering . . . implies a process in which something that happened within the brain is now happening again"* (Levin, 1995, p. 108). There is a patterning that takes place within the brain that becomes a template against which subsequent experience is measured. This process appears to take place at a very primary level. According to Solms (1996): "After certain critical periods, we no longer deliberately analyze each perceptual scene into a variety of significant features, and then deliberately synthesize them into psychologically meaningful wholes" (p. 345). We do not learn simple cause-and-effect rules, but rather we learn contingencies: the conditions under which events are likely to occur (Kandel, 1999). We learn expectancies and then "we project our expectations onto the perceptual scene, in the form of complex representations, and we only adjust these projections if our expectations are not met" (Solms, 1996, p. 345).

These expectations are built up from our earliest preverbal experiences as we begin to organize the world from the mass of sensations we experience internally and externally. Initially, the sensations may be distinguished by qualitative aspects, such as rhythmicity, pleasurability, or familiarity. Over time, it is the patterns themselves to which we respond. These patterns give order and meaning to our experiences and, in turn, affect what is perceived to be useful information or, alternatively, warded off as "noise" or "threat." Ultimately, our sensations become organized into complex narratives of self, other, and world, mediated by the rules of language (Solms, 1996).

As symbolic functions develop, they tend to push the more primary, sensory aspects of knowing to the background. These nonverbal understandings still help to organize and shape our understandings but are not necessarily accessible to conscious awareness. This is efficient, as we can grapple with a great deal of complexity in this fashion, but it can also cause problems when we find ourselves moved in maladaptive or counterproductive ways. At times, we experience these less conscious knowings as "intuition": a sense of patterned order that we understand at a very primary level but may not be able to articulate in words.

This type of patterned awareness seems to be multimodal in nature. If we attend carefully, at times we can translate the patterns we have observed and encoded (in whatever modality) into their verbal counterpart. These basic patterns become units of meaning, which may be transposed from one modality to another and yet be inherently recognizable in terms of their fundamental meanings (Charles, 2002a). Words then enable us to better organize and more effectively communicate these understandings.

Affect is an important way of registering patterns. It has long been noted for its signal functions (Freud, 1926), which provide cues for danger but also perpetuate the illusion of danger when it has passed. "Affect, fundamentally, is about patterns of light and dark, crescendo and decrescendo: expectations, meetings, and disappointments. We carry these patterns within us beyond what may be 'known' about them in any given instance" (Charles, 1999a, p. 19). Affect provides an experiential sense of knowing: a resonance to an important pattern needing our attention.

Through our own affective (countertransference) experiences, we begin to recognize patterns in our interactions with our patients (we discuss countertransference in greater detail in the next chapter). We may encounter these patterns in highly individualized and personalized ways—as in dream fragments or recurrent themes. Over time, the patterns begin to take the form of recognizable symbols that we know through their affective configurations. We can then begin to notice equivalent configurations in the imagery, metaphors, or experiences of the person that are composed of similar patterns in different keys, tones, or modalities.

To the extent that our knowing is nonverbal, it is often difficult to hold meanings in mind, much less communicate them. Free associations on the part of both patient and therapist then offer opportunities to build metaphors together that mark important thematic and affective patterns. Although we listen most pointedly to the patient's own associations, we often find that an image or thought will rise to the surface of our own conscious awareness that provides a useful metaphor that captures some important essence of the topic at hand. These metaphors may be broadly consensual or may be idiosyncratic, built on the themes, values, and understandings of our work together. These in turn, are filtered through whatever meanings had been taken in by the patient through his or her family and the culture at large.

The parent's reality inevitably constrains the child's reality. We take in a worldview that is heavily filtered by the views of our parents and extended family and community network. This includes the affective world, which is colored and constrained by our interactions with those around us. Just as resilience and adaptability can be built in through attuned parenting, so too affective limitations can also be passed along. The inhibitions limiting the affective experience of the parent tend to become restrictions on the child as well. Our world is inevitably modeled on the one we have known. Even when the child rejects the limitations of the parent, he or she may still be limited by them (Shabad, 1993). This can confound reality considerably, as we reject the other in principle while also forming ourselves according to the patterns they have set down. As Shabad (1993) describes, the dissimilarity of content often masks the similarity of structure in these types of reenactments.

As therapists, we tend to configure ourselves according to the patterns of our patients' modes of being in the world. What has been termed *empathy* may be seen as a complex attempt to configure ourselves affectively to the inner workings of an other's being. In this way, we learn to resonate with the particular nuances of that individual's experience of their inner and outer worlds. We are imperfect instruments at best and yet our attempts to "tune" ourselves in their key provides a bridge that helps us to understand one another at a very profound level. Many authors have explored how innate and interactive factors inform the prosodies of interpersonal behavior (see, e.g., Knoblauch, 2000; La Barre, 2001). The ability to tune one's self to the other has its origins within the family, in the early interactions between caretaker and child that become prototypical "dance steps" guiding subsequent interactions (Freud, 1921; Bion, 1961; Charles, 1999b). For some, attunement has been a pleasurable experience, whereas for others it has been learned out of the necessity of having to be vigilant for signs of attack.

We all tend to take on roles in accordance with the configurations defined in our families of origin. The family constellation itself becomes a pattern that prescribes and proscribes future development (Charles, 1999b). The self is constructed through our interactions with others, so that we come to know ourselves through the interplay of our parents' reality onto our own experience (Bollas, 1992). In this way, repetitive themes of both family and culture become patterns that are transmitted across the generations (Shabad, 1993; Charles, 2000).

There are continuing tensions between our attempts to identify and disidentify with parent and sibling representations. The assumption of these roles entails a disowning of aspects of self that have been defined as "not me" within that relationship. As facets of self become not-known, they also become less accessible, making it difficult to use or develop the disowned faculty. In this way, we cripple ourselves through our blindness to parts of ourselves that are beyond our view. Disowned aspects of self are often integrated at a very primitive level, which further compounds their relative inaccessibility (Bion, 1967b).

Patterned experiences often propel our movements in complex ways that may be difficult to discern and yet our ability to discern the patterns can offer profound opportunities for growth. One way in which pattern manifests itself in therapy is in the transference. As therapists, we begin to notice that we seem to be experienced in ways that are incongruent to our own ideas as to who we are or how we are behaving. This lack of congruity offers us important information as to the other person's expectations of what they will encounter in relationships.

One useful way of framing these incongruities has been offered by Racker (1972), in his discussion of concordant and complementary identifications. With *concordant* identifications, we experience empathically what it might be like to be the other person. With *complementary* identifications, we find ourselves cast in the role of the "Other." Either of these positions may be more or less ego syntonic, depending on the role we are invited to play. The complementary role can offer some life-saving distance from a particularly difficult morass in which the patient is embroiled, but can also demand that we sit in very uncomfortable positions as a perpetrator or harsh, critical object. If we can avoid trying to extricate ourselves from uncomfortable roles in which we have been cast, we have an opportunity to better understand where the person gets stuck in his relationships. This perspective helps us to identify the part we are playing in the person's psychic reality in the moment and thereby illuminate the patterns with an immediacy that can be extremely useful. This insight enables us to more effectively communicate our understandings of the patterns at play in ways that might be not only meaningful but also more helpful than hurtful.

Optimally, these understandings—or interpretations—offer the other person an opportunity to "see" from a new vantage point. This provides what is called in literature a "foregrounding" process, in which our habitual view is jarred sufficiently that we might see anew from another perspective (Miall and Kuiken, 1994). It is this enlargement of perspective that enables us to catch a glimpse of disjunctions between reality as we experience it and other possible views. This disjunction offers a bit of respite from the intensity of the affect, which in turn helps us to understand the symmetrization rather than merely being traumatized by it.

Let me give you an example. I worked with a young woman I called Sophia (Charles, 1999b). For Sophia, the pattern that she had learned to identify as "mother" took the form of powerful and hostile critical beings whose reality always prevailed over her own. Psychic survival had been predicated on Sophia's ability to scan with extreme vigilance for that particular pattern in her environment. When she encountered a person who seemed to be configured in that way, she would assume the complementary pattern, which she called "lying low." Hiding in that way ensured her survival but at a very high price to her sense of self. In quite profound ways, Sophia found herself reconfigured in the presence of dangerous others. After accommodating to the dangerous "mother" in this way, Sophia would feel lost, dissociated, and distant. She longed to be able to maintain herself in the presence of these powerful others but despaired that this would ever occur.

Initially, we encountered the dangerous mother in characters drawn from her life outside of the consulting room. It was inevitable, however, that we would eventually encounter the feared mother in our work together, so that we could learn that we could be present with her without being annihilated. In order to prepare ourselves for moving into such treacherous territory, it was crucial that I be able to attune to Sophia sufficiently that I could help her to encounter her fears without dissociating. This attunement was facilitated by my ability to read the nonverbal elements as indicators of transference reactions that were affecting Sophia's ability to be present in the moment.

Being able to track ebbs and flows in the quality of Sophia's presence and absence through my own sensory and affective experiences in our sessions became an important part of the treatment. Over time, I began to notice that it was when Sophia was most angry that she was most likely to become remote. Communicating these impressions to Sophia helped her to become more aware of her own affect. Most particularly, she began to be aware of how profoundly she would lose herself in a given moment. This growing capacity to track her own withdrawal helped her to attenuate this tendency and to also be more mindful of the danger to which she was responding. Over time, I began to notice subtle and yet palpable differences in the quality of Sophia's presence in our sessions, as she became better able to tolerate her affect and to interpret it as a signal inviting attention rather than avoidance.

In this way, my attunement to Sophia's affect helped her to more clearly notice and track her own affect. My ability to make sense of her affective responses in terms of her history and how it becomes reenacted helped her to become more aware of, and thereby less reflexively reactive to, factors that inhibited her from being present in the moment. These factors tended to stem from prohibitions and inhibitions she had taken in through her experiences with her mother. For example, Sophia's mother had worried about her daughter's appetites. As a result, Sophia experienced her desires as repugnant and dangerous. Becoming aware of how reflexively she would inhibit her own desires helped Sophia to encounter them and to better acknowledge and come to terms with them. This awareness helped her to desymmetrize herself from her projections of the other's view, which enabled her to better appreciate how profoundly she patterned herself and her behavior in accordance with her projections regarding the deprecating and rejecting mother.

Even Sophia's experience of herself as a physical being was patterned by her mother's views. For many years, Sophia had felt as though she were out of touch with her body. She told me that her mother saw her as "too big" and had therefore restricted her eating, making bodily needs both vitally important to fill and also so shameful that they were in many ways below conscious awareness. My awareness of her corporeal and sensory absence became an invitation to Sophia to become more interested in attending to her own bodily cues, needs, and experience, rather than viewing them as something alien to suppress or control.

Sophia had maintained her equilibrium by rigorously controlling her eating, in tacit acceptance of her mother's negative view of Sophia's shape and size. Her growing ability to acknowledge and speak to her shame and the resulting dissociation from her body, however, helped Sophia to achieve a greater comfort and fluidity with both the inner and outer experiences of her corporeal self. As she faced her fears of annihilation (patterned after those of her parents), Sophia found herself to be moored, not so uncomfortably nor dangerously, in her own body; in her own reality.

As Sophia became more present in her experiences, she was also better able to utilize the signal functions of her affect. This helped her to encounter difficult situations outside of our work and to attain mastery without losing touch with her own feelings and interests. In particular, as Sophia began to pay more attention to her experiences of becoming lost, she was better able to encounter the "mother" without becoming lost and overwhelmed. Having internalized a pattern of a good-enough mother through our work together seemed to help her to keep her bearings in the face of the feared critical mother.

Sophia's ability to face her own demons changed the expected pattern. Avoidance tends to perpetuate our fears. If we can actually encounter the feared situation, we can begin to get our bearings and to notice discrepancies between the anticipated fear and the encountered actuality. Breaking through her preconceptions of "mother" enabled Sophia to also break through the disjunctive ideas that had arisen regarding self versus mother. Her mother had taken on such a negative valence in her mind that Sophia was unable to even see parts of her self that were like her mother. My ability to accept both the sameness and the difference helped Sophia to acknowledge the powerful parts of her self that at times frighten and intimidate others, while also being aware of the disjunctions. For Sophia, these similarities were tempered by the greater empathy and self- and other-awareness that make her unlike her mother.

As aspects of self become entrenched, they become self, as though they were innate characteristics: the "ground" or given, which may be struggled with or moderated but always as if with something inherently fixed and unchangeable. The resulting dichotomies are such that any middle ground becomes essentially unseen. As the self becomes divided into the provinces of "me" and "not me," whatever is defined as not me is not seen within the bounds of the self but only outside. At a deeply unconscious level, we play out the patterns that have become literally incomprehensible to us, in our attempts to master the trauma associated with them. However, until we can understand what it is we are trying to play out, the attempts tend to be ill-fated. Once again, the primary purpose of the enactments would seem to be to "mark the spot."

Ultimately, our ambivalence and dichotomizations are often worked out through transference enactments. Being able to de-idealize the therapist is an important part of being able to accept the self as a whole, complex being with disparate pieces that need not be disowned in order to attain equilibrium. Good enough does not mean good. It is important to avoid becoming engaged with the patient in a splitting process. Although it is important for them to be able to see us as relatively benign, the important issue is that we are able to detoxify what seems to be impossibly bad, by looking at it.

With Sophia, as with Kate (see chapter 4) it was crucial to be able to de-idealize me sufficiently that we could each have a full range of "good" and "bad" aspects, rather than believing that these could be split between self and other. For Kate, the vehicle for this resolution came through finally acknowledging her anger at me, whereas for Sophia it came through expressing her anger in the session and discovering that she could do so without inviting retaliation. In each case, it was important to affirm that anger could be present in the room without anyone having to be annihilated.

With Sophia, an essential part of the transference was the need to keep me in the position of the "good" mother lest I become the "bad" mother. This stance encouraged the perpetuation of the split between ostensibly good and bad aspects of herself as well. An important step in resolving this split came during a time when Sophia was extremely angry with me. She projected this anger onto me and became extremely agitated and preoccupied by it, insisting that I must be angry as well. Sophia repeatedly confronted me on this issue and appeared to be trying to provoke me into an attack.

I considered my feelings very carefully because I was certainly aroused but did not experience this arousal as anger but rather as frustration. Although I was frustrated by the impasse in which we found ourselves, I did not experience myself as angry. I wondered silently whether I was merely softening my feelings as a way of staying within the parameters of my ideas of the "good analyst." After some reflection, I told Sophia that I did not feel angry but rather felt frustrated at the impasse we were experiencing.

As we continued to process this interaction, however, it became clear to me that what was important was for Sophia to be able to discover that I could be angry without attacking or destroying her. At this juncture, it was important for me to be able to separate the transference (Sophia's experience of me as angry) from whatever feelings I might actually have in the moment and to stay with the transference. This helped me to keep my interventions in line with Sophia's needs rather than serving my own by moving defensively toward "clarifying" the "reality" of the moment (e.g., see Gill, 1979) and serving my own transferences regarding what it means to be a "good therapist." I told Sophia that I thought that this issue of anger was important because she needed to learn that one can be angry without attacking. This was what she seemed to be trying to resolve in bringing forward this issue.

In confronting my anger, Sophia was able to see that one can be angry without doing harm. In confronting internally my own resistance to being seen as angry, I was able to allow Sophia to face the feared object and survive the encounter. By allowing Sophia to experience me as angry but not retaliative or deadly, we were able to create a situation in which she could encounter experientially the notion that one could be angry without losing touch with whatever is positive in a relationship and without losing the relationship itself. We were able to talk about the impasse we had reached and our respective frustrations without needing to attack one another.

For Sophia, encountering the "bad object" aspects of me provided a means for also beginning to integrate split aspects of self. However, this necessitated that I encounter my own bad object aspects as well. We are confronted once again with our ambivalence; there is a part of ourselves that inevitably works toward health, wholeness, and understanding, even as we run in the other direction. For the therapist, this poses particular difficulties. Although it can feel good to sit on the positive side of the split, it also feels pressured and immobilizing, ultimately as persecutory as sitting on the bad side of the split. Real growth can only occur through acknowledgement of both the desire to sit on one side and the reality that one cannot adaptively do so. This acceptance and resignation resolves the schism and brings us to the depressive position, from which point we might move forward. The idea of transference helps us to keep in mind the inevitable mismatches between our conceptions of self and other and to actively seek out and attempt to understand these.

In this way, the idea of transference also invites us to explore more explicitly the ways in which important experiences and patterns of relationship provide themes that organize our sense of who we are and how the world is structured. For Simon, for example, whose mother committed suicide when he was 15 months old, absence profoundly shaped not only his sense of mother but also his expectations of relationships more generally. His ambivalence over his own relational needs was further complicated by his difficulties in identifying with and feeling valued by his father. Simon found it difficult to find himself within the very real constraints and deprivations of his history.

The metaphor of "patterns" was an ongoing and important theme in our work together. In our attempts to understand where he found himself caught, we found ourselves playing out in the transference some of the important themes from Simon's life.

Loss, in particular, was difficult for Simon to tolerate. It reminded him at a very deep and profound level of the loss of his mother. The reluctance to face the intensity of this loss was exacerbated by the intensity of his longings for "mother." This made the transference dynamic particularly precarious as we began to confront his ambivalence over his longings for and fears of closeness as they played out in our relationship. We encountered this issue most pointedly as Simon neared graduation from university. Simon seemed to find it difficult to face the imminence of endings, but rather seemed to be moving away affectively as a way of avoiding the reality of loss.

I suggested that he had hoped not to have to face the pain of leaving and yet there was important work to be done in facing that loss together, in a way that had never been possible for him with previous losses, particularly that of his mother. It seemed to be important to him to be able to just vanish. This urge to disappear, in my mind, seemed to carry the image of his mother. Disappearing was not only a way of avoiding being left but also of trying to find her. Simon did not understand what I was trying to say, and so I said that there are times when we identify with people as a way of making sense of them, as when we play "dress-up" as children—as a way of knowing/being our parents—and that we do it in other ways as well. We try them on for size, as a way of trying to know them from the inside out.

"It was a way for you to keep her with you," I said. Simon was silent for some time, digesting my words. The air was very heavy with the enormity of his mother's abandonment. I said that it is terrifying to all of us to lose our mothers, yet most of us are able to re-find enough of her to enable us to go on.

"So I keep looking for her?" he asked.

"She wasn't there to be re-found," I replied, "and becoming her has been a way of not feeling the pain of that."

Simon's alignment with mother was profoundly patterned after his experience of being and not being with her, which he kept replaying as a way of trying both to undo the loss and to attain mastery over the pain. In addition to replaying and reworking relational patterns, we also identify and disidentify with *traits* of important others. These qualities or traits become sorted into what is seen as "like me" or "not like me." We learn to pattern ourselves after those significant others from whom we have learned what it means to be a human being and to make one's way in the world.

For example, Simon had never really identified with his father but rather had always felt distanced from him. He was much more aware of dissimilarities to his father than he was of similarities. At a certain point in our work together, however, Simon began to talk about ways in which he found himself configuring to the pattern of his father; in particular, to his father's worrying. Simon had become aware of his own worrying and was uncertain as to how much of this was his own and how much configured to his father. I suggested that this worrying was a way of aligning with his father; of being with him and of being him.

We run into this kind of equivalence or condensation of meanings frequently in this work and can easily become lost in it. At those times, a bit of understanding can help us get our bearings without losing whatever opportunities might be inherent in the moment. There are several conceptualizations that I have found particularly helpful in understanding this type of equivalence. First, there is the importance of being aware that meanings change depending on the context, the history, and the intent (Bion, 1977). This helps us to "mark the spot"; to wonder about the meaning of a given word or phrase at any particular moment, rather than presuming that our understanding is the same as that of the other person or the same as it was at another point in the treatment.

As Winnicott (1971) notes, the analyst who "knows too much" destroys the patient's creativity. Bion (1977) refers to this in terms of "saturating" an element or a space through our belief that whatever we already know is more important than whatever we do not know. For example, Simon's assumption that he was not like his father made it difficult for him to notice the ways in which he was like him. This made fundamental aspects of self and experience relatively inaccessible and incomprehensible to him.

It is important to note that we have just moved from a discussion of equivalences (failure to note dissimilarities) to disjunctions (failure to note similarities). We can see here how it becomes difficult for Simon to maintain his bearings as the affect intensifies. At this level of intensity, the therapist in that moment becomes the mother, and the patient has difficulty distinguishing between the two. Even though at some level they are clearly not the same person, they may be experienced as such. As Simon contemplates leaving me and our work, I become the mother who abandons him endlessly. Our task is then to focus on the asymmetry—the differences within the sameness—so that we can think about and come to understand the intrusion, rather than merely being overwhelmed and overcome by it.

Looking at Simon's dilemma through the framework of Matte-Blanco's (1975) bi-logic, we can see that experiences of loss or potential loss were too similar to his early abandonment to enable him to easily keep his bearings. As affect intensifies, it becomes more difficult to think in rational terms. As Simon and I attempted to find our way through these difficult spaces, Matte-Blanco's theory of bi-logic provided us with a structure within which we could begin more constructively to "hold in mind" what had seemed inconceivable because thinking about it had become too painful. These conceptualizations also provided me with a framework through which to begin to communicate to Simon some of my understandings of the patterns that defined and proscribed his experience. The unconscious patterning had been so strong in this young man, and so willfully denied, that he had little way of seeing the forces that moved him so vitally.

In my work with both Simon and Sophia, my ability to keep these ideas in mind provided me with important conceptual anchors through which to find my own guideposts as we immersed ourselves in at times blindingly murky waters. It was my understanding of what Matte-Blanco (1975, 1988) terms the realms of "symmetry" and "asymmetry" that helped me to put before Simon patterns of his existence in a fashion that brought them into striking relief for him, whereby he, too, could see and struggle with them without being crushed by them.

Being able to see the pattern helped to relieve the terrible weight of the repetition. In turn, being able to see the intensity of the affect as a chain to the pattern helped Simon to separate the two enough to be able to envision alternatives. These conceptual anchors helped him to think more fully about his experience, enabling him to more clearly discriminate, in Matte-Blanco's terms, the asymmetry of past and present. This enhanced clarity enabled Simon to envision the future without becoming lost in the condensation of present into past.

Understanding is facilitated by an environment in which both anxiety and ambiguity can be contained. For both Simon and Sophia, this containment helped to relieve the intensity of the affect sufficiently that they were able to think more constructively. Each was able to experience sameness while also making important distinctions between self and other, and among past, present, and future.

The ability to hold in mind both similarity and distinction helps us to see and make sense of fundamental patterns organizing and constraining our experiences of self and other. These include the relational patterns that come to obscure the particulars of a current relationship that would be useful to be able to take into account but have become clouded by experience and expectation. For both Simon and Sophia, greater insight into the overlays of their own transference patterns enabled them to tolerate the discomfort of the work sufficiently to gain a real and life-enhancing understanding that furthered their development in profound ways.

The capacity for understanding the regularities within one's own emotional functioning is crucial for the development of an autonomous self, capable of real and meaningful engagement with others. From these ensues, as Winnicott (1971) describes so beautifully, the capacity to survive.

12

Empathic Resonance
The Role of
Countertransference

OUR MOST PRIMARY understandings are nonverbal. Although language helps us to grapple with complexity, it can also obscure some of our more primary understandings of self and world, which are based, not on rational logic, but rather on our deepest sense of what it means to be human. These primary understandings are derived from the regularities and disregularities of sensory experience that are integrated as *patterns* that come to have meanings over time, whether or not we are conscious of them (Charles, 2002a).

From our earliest moments of being, we begin to develop a "language of the body" (Charles, 2002a). These primary ways of knowing self and other continue to have an impact on our understandings, even as they shift to the background with the advent of verbal language. The interactive rhythmicity of primary sensations provides the context in which basic antitheses, such as light and dark, comfort and discomfort, come to order the universe. This dialectic provides the building blocks of experience, through which the world is "decoded" (Mancia, 1981). Words give us a way of organizing our experiences, but they also distance us from primary sensory experience. In this way, words provide a safe container for our anxieties, but they can also distort experience, making it more remote and less accessible. In therapy, there is an ongoing tension between the need to provide sufficient containment to be able to look at what troubles us and the need not to lose touch with the reality of the experience as lived.

Many memories are not encoded in words, but rather as body memories. The language of the body is built on the patternings of experience that become basic preconceptions of "the way things are," even though we might not be able to name or describe them in verbal terms. Developmental theorists and observers of infant behavior (see, e.g., Stern, 1985) describe an innate facility for intramodal or cross-modal processing. Information taken in through one sensory modality is digested and then recommunicated through another modality, retaining in some essential way the primary pattern of the information. These transactions are nonverbal, but highly coordinated (Beebe and Lachmann, 1998), and appear to be processed much more quickly than verbal language.

In this type of reciprocal interaction, each person's actions are continually modified by those of the other, in a system Fogel (1992) describes as "coregulation." The partners do not match one another exactly, but rather each anticipates the movements of the other in reciprocal patternings that tend to move in the same direction affectively in the form of what Stern (1985) calls "matching the gradient." In this way, primary experiences are translated between self and other in dyadic communications of prosody, touch, and rhythmicity. Affective resonance becomes a palpable form of intercommunication, directing and modifying thought and behavior. Although we tend to hold nonrational ways of knowing suspect, our intuitions may be viewed as composite indicators gleaned from all previous experience.

The good-enough mother (in the generic sense of the primary caretaker) feeds back to the child digested or metabolized versions of his or her communications. This empathic resonance provides a basic sense of being understood. It also provides containment of the child's affect, keeping it within tolerable bounds. This process of what Stern (1985) terms *affective attunement* depends on the quality of the parent's emotional responsiveness; the ability to respond sensitively and empathically to the child. This facility allows for elaborate interchanges of complex meanings without the necessity of verbal language.

Our capacity for intra- or cross-modal processing enables us to take in nonverbal information and to process it interactively. At some level, it is the pattern of the information that is being processed, integrated, and reflected back in a form that confirms, validates, and moderates the experience. This moderation may take the form of titrating intense affect or, alternatively, amplifying responsiveness where that might be more appropriate.

Translating this into the clinical setting, the clinician needs to be able to attune him- or herself to the patient sufficiently to be able to "read" the affect and have a sense of when to amplify and when to titrate. The patient who is overwhelmed by affect may need sufficient soothing to be able to begin to think about the distress, whereas the individual who is out of touch with emotions might need to be able to encounter the emotions via the other.

We can see this type of interplay perhaps most clearly within the mother–infant dyad, as we watch, for example, an infant's expression of distress mirrored initially by the mother's tone and then attenuated slowly toward a more soothing tone. The initial mirroring meets the child where he or she is, providing a sense of feeling understood; a basic sense of feeling "held." Following this initial mirroring with an attenuation modulates the basic pattern of the experience, thereby easing the child's distress. Over time, this regulatory process becomes internalized so that the child can attenuate his or her own experience, without the parent's actual presence.

In the clinical setting, we would like to be able to keep the affect within tolerable levels, so that individuals can experience their feelings without becoming overwhelmed. This enables them to better learn from their own experience, which is the best reference point we can have. We would like patients to feel sufficiently safe that they might be able to tolerate being where they want to go. If we see the goal of therapy as greater understanding, we want to be able to use as many of the resources available in order to further that understanding. One of our most important resources is our own affect.

Optimally, we learn to read affect like a signal, continually giving us feedback as to our emotional status at any given moment. If we are able to notice our affect at relatively low levels, we can act accordingly and are more likely to be able to keep the affect within tolerable limits. Spikes of affect then become signals telling us that something is wrong that needs our immediate attention. This signaling system is extremely useful when it is working well. It helps us to index both quality and intensity so that we can mark pleasurable and displeasurable experiences. In turn, this indexing helps us to organize our understandings of where and how pleasurable and displeasurable experiences are obtained.

Overwhelming affect is not useful for its signal functions, but rather is experienced as trauma, which inhibits cognitive functions and impedes adaptation more generally (Krystal, 1988). Affect that is not kept within tolerable limits is extremely stressful and overwhelms our systems. Unattended distress tends to surface as symptoms, which register for us the distress but may cause further problems in the form of somatic disturbances or avoidant behaviors, such as overeating or substance abuse.

It is particularly important for therapists to be aware of their own affect and to be able to read subtleties and changes in the affective field over time in the therapeutic process. In our work with patients, affective patterns are exchanged through complex sensory interchanges that come to carry multiple meanings over time. Each person has their own dialect; their way of communicating subtlety and nuance, value and meaning. We resonate to differences in affective tones and to other qualities that may be communicated through the rhythmicity of gesture or the prosodies of speech. Within the dyad, these resonances carry meanings that are communicated back and forth at very primary levels, often far beyond conscious awareness. Our ability to resonate affectively to these nonverbal elements helps us to mark, and then to put into words, elements that had not been available to conscious awareness but rather had formed part of what Bollas (1987) refers to as the *unthought known*: aspects of awareness that are so integral to our sense of self and world that they remain unnoticed.

Our primary instrument for encountering and reading these nonverbal elements is our own affective responsiveness; our countertransference. This view of countertransference is consistent with Heimann's (1950) definition, in which it is depicted as roughly synonymous with empathy. In contrast, others, such as Reich (1951) point toward the more problematic responses of the therapist, which are based on unresolved conflicts or needs (Brenner, 1985). Although countertransference can certainly pose problems within the treatment, over time clinicians have also come to appreciate the extraordinary utility of being able to assess and evaluate one's own responses in the moment (Heimann, 1950). This attunement helps us to track, in our own sensoria, changes in the affective field. As we act on the basis of our conjectures and pay close attention to the consequences, we gain a better understanding of how to interpret various sensations we encounter in the work.

Part of what we are tracking are the interactions between ourselves and the other person. These interactions are not merely verbal but also take place at the level of gesture, intonation, and rhythmicity. If we are willing to take them seriously, nonverbal patterned movements offer entry points into the interactive meanings being established in the dyad. I have described these interactions as a form of "nonphysical touch" that communicates at a quite profound level what it means to be with another person at a given point in time (Charles, 2002a).

There is an interactive rhythmicity to these interactions that provides information and also offers an opportunity to have a more direct impact in the moment. For example, I have noticed reciprocal movements between myself and my patients (as I rub my fingers or reposition my body, for example), and have wondered to what extent my movements have affected their own and vice versa. At times, the reciprocal rhythms seem to have a soothing quality, and I have wondered whether I am providing needed soothing or whether I am avoiding moving further into treacherous waters that might actually be important to encounter.

People vary in terms of their comfort and discomfort at being in close contact with another person. Keeping in mind the metaphor of the container and the contained, we can think about the difficulties of providing containment for one for whom contact with others has seemed treacherous. The intensity of the intimacy of the therapeutic environment can feel quite dangerous to someone for whom "touch" (in the nonphysical sense I am using here) has been problematic. Many people come to us having had their boundaries impinged upon in one sense or another. Whether this has been an actual physical intrusion or an overriding of psychic boundaries or ego functions, contact with another person becomes inherently problematic.

As therapists, we like to think of ourselves as being supportive. For many of our patients, however, our "supportiveness" can feel intrusive or frightening. It is important to be able to move beyond our more generic ideas about how things should feel and focus instead on the individual's actual responses. We can obtain preliminary information from the person's history that can alert us as to how their interpersonal world is configured, but it is really only in our moment-by-moment interactions with them that we have a more palpable sense of the emotional realities of that world. Our attunement to the affect of the other person provides us with important information as to the meanings and feelings for them in a given interaction.

For example, in my work with Hallie, my emotional resonance was an essential part of being able to establish a relationship. Our relationship was always tentative at best. She often seemed to me like a startled doe, ready to run. Hallie described her mother as extremely narcissistic, intrusive, and overbearing. It sounded as though Hallie's mother always needed to be the center of attention. Her needs were paramount in the family, and the unwritten rule enforced accommodation to the mother, first and foremost. This reversal of the traditional parent–child roles made Hallie feel responsible for her mother's emotional well-being. Tracking her mother's affect thus became an essential part of Hallie's own well-being. She learned to keep an external appearance of calm and contentment in place to hide whatever turbulence lay beneath. Being with others had always felt as though it must come at the price of being herself, making it difficult for her to find a comfortable place for herself within the world of peers as well.

This emphasis on external image over internal experience created particular dilemmas in our work. Hallie was very good at pretending that everything was fine and often would only let me know of her distress when the session was over. At times of most dire distress, she would leave a message on my machine saying that she had decided to discontinue the treatment altogether. Then I would know that I had failed her in some essential way. Responding to these calls let Hallie know that I did indeed take her feelings and well-being seriously, which enabled her to return to our work.

It became clear to me that I would need to be very attuned to Hallie's affect in the moment in order to avoid these types of disruption and repair sequences (Lachmann and Beebe, 1996). However, the sequences themselves provided Hallie with needed reassurance that repair was possible. In some ways, being able to play out this pattern of disruption and repair may have been the most important issue.

This paradox brings us quite pointedly to the issue of mistakes. There is a part of us that would like to be able to avoid startle and disruption, and yet these sequences are important parts of the therapeutic process. Our willingness to make mistakes—to be wrong—not only provides a venue through which we might learn something new but also provides an important model for adaptive living. In some sense, the term itself is often a misnomer, in that so-called *mistakes* are often more productive than the most erudite interpretation. Often, what we term a mistake is an inevitable bumbling through some dark corridor that we need to explore more thoroughly.

I worked with one woman, for example, who would never merely accept any statement I had made. Grace would invariably respond with a "no" and then go on to agree substantially with whatever I had said. My initial reaction was to become very invested in trying to say things in a better way—the "right" way—so that I might receive a "yes" rather than a "no."

Over time, I came to appreciate that the "no" represented an important assertion of Grace's need to put her own stamp on her reality. The negation provided a means by which Grace was able to make my words her own. It was important for me to be able to sit back, metaphorically, and allow Grace to take her rightful place as the arbiter of her own reality. In this way, to the extent that we are able to offer tentatively a potential reading of a situation, we invite the other person to join with us in trying to understand.

A focus on understanding helps us to play a bit more in the process, without feeling so persecuted by our ideas about "right answers" that we become inhibited and unable to think creatively. Being able to sit back and watch the flow of the session while also being a participant is a crucial task for us in making use of our countertransference reactions. Being attuned to our own affective signals helps us track the interactive quality of the sessions in such a way that we can build resilience. This resilience then helps us each to tolerate our lack of understanding so that we can build an environment in which we can more freely play with ideas in a mutual search for understanding.

13

Play

Opening Up the Space

ONE OF THE CAPACITIES we try to build in this work is the ability to play with ideas and meanings as a way of opening up possibilities. If we are able to get a bit of distance from "Reality" with a capital R, we can begin to consider alternatives, to play with them and try them on for size. This flexibility depends on our ability to be present in the moment; to move more fully into the realm that both Bion and Winnicott describe as one of "being."

These theorists realized how important it is for the therapist to be present in the moment. This presence becomes a crucial reference point that helps to develop that capacity in the patient as well. Our willingness to confront uncomfortable moments in the work and to acknowledge difficult truths (and not turn away from them) conveys a message of hope as we try to make sense of whatever seems to be out of reach.

We often fill in these difficult moments as a way of not having to confront them. Opposing this urge, Bion (1967a) encourages us to renounce memory or desire, so that we are better able to observe what is actually occurring within the hour rather than saturating the space arbitrarily with our "understanding," our hopes, or our fears. Winnicott (1971), too, cautions us to avoid filling the space with *our* ideas, so that we leave room for the patient to generate his or her own. He says: "premature interpretation . . . annihilates the creativity of the patient and is traumatic in the sense of being against the maturational process" (p. 117). Our discomfort with not knowing can encourage us to be didactic, leading to learning facts rather than to any real understanding. In practice, says Winnicott (1971), "even the right explanation is ineffectual. The person we are trying to help needs a new experience" (p. 55). Ultimately, we want people to be able to develop ideas and theories about who they are and how they function that are sufficiently grounded in their own experiences that these ideas might actually be useful to them.

When we take our own theories too seriously, they become preconceptions that obscure rather than illuminate. In this way, they impede our ability to observe what might actually be taking place. Bion (1977) speaks to this issue with characteristic grace and humor: "As I became more able to silence my prejudices, I also became able to be aware of the evidence that was there rather than to regret the evidence that was not" (p. 22). To some extent, we need to be willing to cast ourselves adrift from our theories in order to discover when, whether, and in what ways these theories apply. Otherwise, it becomes too easy merely to affirm what we already believe we know rather than learning anything from our actual experiences. This hazard makes it important to find ways of disentangling perception from apperception.

Our expectancies and defenses inevitably color our perceptions. This dilemma, however, reached monumental proportions in my work with a young man I call Conrad (Charles, 2004). With Conrad, I could see how the fusion of perception with preconception became a paranoid–schizoid reality in which reality testing was at times highly obstructed. It was often difficult to see the whole out of fear of finding the "fear become reality" that seemed to lie in wait. This dynamic made it difficult even to engage with Conrad as a whole person, for that would have meant acknowledging the devalued aspects of self.

Conrad's sensors avoided any encounters with his devalued qualities, out of fear that this implicit acknowledgment would annihilate his sense of value as a person. In order to escape this gridlock, we needed a way of understanding the whole person that was not inherently intolerable. We needed a way of moving out of the two-dimensional space of the paranoid–schizoid dichotomous reality into a three-dimensional space in which we might be able to envision alternatives.

As discussed in chapter 3, Bion (1965) suggests that it is largely in the realm of metaphor that complex meanings are most productively communicated. Metaphor allows us some distance in which we might play with reality by encountering difficult truths without feeling as though we are in imminent danger of being annihilated by them. This affords us an opportunity for mastery as we begin to explore various truths with another person.

For Winnicott (1971), the experience of mastery arises from our ability to be able to play with another person:

> The thing about playing is always the precariousness of the interplay of personal psychic reality and the experience of the control of actual objects. This is the precariousness of magic itself, magic that arises in intimacy, in a relationship that is being found to be reliable [p. 47].

It is in this type of relationship that we can perhaps learn to be *ourselves* more truly and more creatively.

Real creativity also entails being able to integrate our destructiveness, so that we can be in relationship and also be separate. For the therapist, Winnicott (1971) suggests, the capacity to survive means the capacity to not retaliate. "Without the experience of maximum destructiveness (object not protected) the subject never places the analyst outside and therefore can never do more than experience a kind of self-analysis, using the analyst as a projection of a part of the self" (p. 91). Although self-analysis has its benefits, it is important to believe that one can encounter the other without either person needing to be destroyed. This faith helps us to have greater assurance in thinking our own thoughts, without quite so much fear that they might not be understood or valued by the other.

As therapists, when we consider speaking, we need to be able to think about whether we are actually adding something or whether we are taking something away. At times, it is important to be able to tolerate our discomfort with our own silence and question to what extent the urge to speak represents an urge to reassure ourselves that we do indeed have something to offer. The resolutions of these gaps carry important meanings regarding our relative faith in the other person's ability to come to his own constructive realizations. Our urge to give more than might be necessary may be a replaying of assumptions the individual has carried with him regarding his own perceived deficiencies. This makes it important to be mindful of whether we are being complicit in affirming this type of negative assumption.

As we reconstructed Conrad's interpersonal world within the consulting room, the issue of what it means to be able to rely on one's own resources was pivotal. His parents' overindulgence seemed to have left him with limited frustration tolerance. This deficit had led to quite striking failures, which fed his narcissistic vulnerabilities and further attenuated the lines between fantasy and reality. Although Conrad seemed to be able to "play" very creatively, he was unable actually to engage in play with others. For Conrad, play was fundamentally private and interactions were predicated on rigid role structures. Conrad had constructed a persona—a public self—that was playful and delightful. He would seem, to even the keen observer, to have not a care in the world. Yet, he was unable, in spite of his obviously superior intellectual capacities, to meet specific developmental challenges; most recently, an inability to pass his classes at university or to seek employment.

Conrad was unable to test in public aspects of self that he privately assumed to be superior. His desire for secrecy, however, only affirmed his fears. Continuing to build fantasies about himself in his internal world, without trying and testing them in the external world, increased the gap between fantasy and reality, thereby affirming his fears and increasing the need for secrecy. Secrecy was so essential to Conrad's well-being that it became increasingly difficult for him even to try anything new or important, lest he fail.

This dilemma severely constricted Conrad's world. The only environments that felt safe were the worlds of family and of the highly structured games Conrad and his friends created by networking their computers. Within these bounded and highly circumscribed realities, Conrad could range relatively freely. Encountering the limits of these worlds, however, was painful.

As we began to explore Conrad's dilemma, it became clear that he was unwilling to be tried in any way that might lead to failure. Paradoxically, however, if his failure was revealed to him in a way that invited understanding, Conrad was intrigued and engaged and could use this information toward further growth. From the right perspective, he could ignore the fact of the failure by focusing very intently on the problem itself and on his ability to resolve it. What he could not tolerate was anything that felt abrupt, that surprised him with awareness of any lack or insufficiency on his part. He could see the "something more" but not the "something less."

Although Conrad appeared to be quite playful and seemed to enjoy his performances, at another level he seemed to be playing a deadly serious game in which survival depended on killing off aspects of self and of self-awareness. When Conrad described his parents, it appeared that they too had delighted in his performances. What they did not seem to have managed, however, was to have helped him develop a tolerance for frustration or failure. This left his capacity for play limited by his ability to achieve sufficient positive mirroring of whatever self he was reflecting. Reality was manageable when it reflected his preferred views or when he could rearrange it sufficiently in his mind to fail to encounter problematic aspects.

Conrad was so unwilling to fail that he created his own system of rules. Whenever he was confronted with a potential failure, he would magically change the rules so that no failure was possible. He could change the rules so quickly that it was often difficult to keep track of what was or was not "true" in any given moment. At times, he would mark the change, pantomiming the shift quite vividly with body motions as though he were steering a car or playing a video game. If confronted, Conrad could freely and pleasantly acknowledge that a changing of the rules was indeed taking place and yet, unless pressed, the previous reality would remain deconstructed.

As this facility with avoidance became more apparent, so did its troublesome aspects. Conrad's awareness of his inability to tolerate whatever was distasteful began to coexist with his remarkable facility for playing with reality. My awareness seemed to mark the spot of the erasure, so that Conrad could not so easily avoid noticing his own avoidance and being troubled by it. It began to be clearer to both of us that this magical capacity for changing the rules was also an evasive defense against growth.

"Ooh, *that's* not good," he would say, his face twisted in thoughtful determination at this puzzle being presented. Conrad seemed to be able to enjoy the challenge as long as he felt able to maintain his sense of his own capacity while encountering the deficit.

My conjecture was that there had been too much accommodation to Conrad as he was growing up, along with very strong rules about what was acceptable and what was unacceptable. This resulted in three dilemmas that seem to have collided like a train wreck, leaving him immobilized with no sense of why this had occurred. This immobilization seemed to validate an underlying sense of worthlessness that coexisted with his grandiose fantasies without any means for integration.

The first dilemma was that Conrad was not able to attack the parent sufficiently to enable him to discover that his mother was neither omniscient nor destructible. The second dilemma seems to have been that he was so bright as a child that he had never learned to tolerate failure but rather became skilled at avoiding any evidence that failure might be forthcoming. The third dilemma was that he was not able to come up to his mother's exacting standards.

All three dilemmas were complicated by Conrad's extraordinary ability to split reality, so that he was able to ignore problems and to disavow his desire to forge his own standards. Not having been able to deidealize his mother, and thereby discover that she could survive this assault, had left him unable to deidealize himself and find that he too could survive. This failure left Conrad in a terrible bind. He could not think about the issues that distressed him most without experiencing overwhelming incapacity and shame. And so he preferred to *not* think about them, which left him unable to discover himself according to his own standards; he was unable to grow up.

For Conrad, blindness became a means for survival. His unwillingness to take responsibility for his actions left him feeling powerless in the real world, forcing him to abdicate developmental tasks and to retreat into the world of fantasy. Fantasy, then, had taken the form described by Winnicott (1971), in which it takes the place of living rather than enriching it. It becomes a dead end rather than providing a means for understanding or growth.

As mentioned previously, Steiner (1985) links this type of avoidance to the oedipal myth, in which blindness becomes a means for denying culpability and responsibility. This reading of the myth also marks the dilemma of trying to build a self while coming up against parental prohibitions against knowing or defining self in any way that might negate or oppose the parental view. Real development depends on our ability to sacrifice the old self (the self we assume our parents had wanted us to be), which is also, at some level, the sacrifice of the parents. This is a terrifying and yet ultimately liberating act that exacts a price, but not so large a price as our failure to meet this challenge.

In our work together, Conrad and I attempted to build a space in which new myths could be made. This required us to come up against the fear that one of us might be destroyed in the process. We needed to be able to discover that we could come up against the other's reality and explore the differences. This ability to consider more freely and then to embrace or discard elements offered the possibility of renouncing some aspects of the myths of childhood by way of building new, more facilitative myths. Building these new myths offered an opportunity for growth, enabling Conrad to integrate disowned parts of himself and to accept himself as the active agent of his own desires.

My awareness of the importance of being able to amend Conrad's myth that he must be hidden in order to be safe kept me searching for ways to engage with him without too much intrusion. For me, it often felt like a game of "Double Dutch" in which I was watching the ropes turn, attempting to attune myself sufficiently to their rhythm to be able to enter into the dance without ending it. To this end, I attempted to join with him in his ambivalence over leaving behind some of the defenses he had built that kept him feeling safe, but also kept him stuck. I also tried to affirm that he might be able to be different from his parents in some ways and also be valued, so that this difference might not be experienced as a devaluation of the parents whose idealization felt so crucial to his well-being and survival.

Entering into the realm of myth with our patients enables us to confront difficult realities within the safety of the displacement. At times, these myths may be quite explicit, as in my work with Elena. We began our journey in the shadow of an archaic murderous mother, encountering images of Medea and her deadly powers (Charles, 2001b). Over time, these images became transmuted and transformed into more benign myths in which the mother could be insufficient without being evil (Charles, 2004).

With Conrad, in contrast, our myths were less sharply defined and yet traversed familiar territory beginning with the sirens who preempted internal control and moving toward narratives in which the *internal* siren calls could be acknowledged. Conrad had created a myth in which he was the hapless victim of a siren who had lured him into temptation. Although this myth left him ostensibly blameless and thereby saved him from devaluation in his mother's eyes, it also left him impotent and unable to become a man. He had no way of reconciling the role of the "good son" with the adult sexuality that he experienced as an unforgivable trespass upon the primal scene.

As Conrad told me this story, he encountered my unwillingness to collude with his myth of redemption through blindness and impotence. I countered his view with one in which he need not be seen as irretrievably damaged for having taken this step toward adulthood. As we began to play with Conrad's myths of sin and redemption, we began to loosen the knots of the paranoid–schizoid reality in which it seemed as though he must somehow undo damage already done. We began to fashion a new myth, one in which he could begin to relinquish the fantasy self rather than so blindly believing in it.

To some extent, Conrad had come to believe that he must be the "darling son" in order to have value. Although this had intrinsic enjoyment for him, it also stifled his development. And so, I attempted to stand with one foot firmly planted in his reality and the other planted in a reality that I posited as only seemingly irreconcilable; one that need not destroy him or his place in the universe but rather might enlarge both. To this end, Conrad's ability to be delighted by surprises that do not overwhelm him was an important resource in our work together. He came to learn and to affirm that the unknown need not be an affirmation of his inherent unworthiness but rather an invitation to grow.

Conrad's actions had the "feel" of play without providing the type of growth we see when play is more firmly grounded. In this way it became more like "fantasying": an empty escape or evasion. This evasion enabled Conrad to derive ostensible support from his family and environment, which helped him to maximize whatever gains he was able to make in the short run but also inhibited his ability to make sustained efforts in our work together. Play had become a destructive activity that took the place of living and affirmed his deepest fears. Our work together helped Conrad to engage more directly with self, other, and world, in part through enlarging and expanding his "myths" so that he was no longer quite so imprisoned by the past. In this way, he was better able to learn from his experience and to begin to bring his creativity to bear in more adaptive, productive, and satisfying ways.

14

Conclusion

WE COME TO THE END of this journey having encountered lots of terms, lots of different ways of conceptualizing these spaces we get into in our work and in our lives. Some of these conceptualizations may resonate for you; some may not. Some meanings may come upon you slowly and enlarge as your own arsenal of experience grows. Most important, I think, is to have a conceptualization that works for you and to be open to revisioning and revising it as new concepts and conceptions intrude.

At a recent conference, I had the opportunity to hear Philip Bromberg talk about his work with difficult patients, and I really had to laugh because he was talking about exactly the same things I was to talk about later that day but in a different language. His views were framed in relational terms; mine in those of Winnicott and Bion. It was reassuring to know that, whatever our language, we were encountering some basic truths that were being affirmed by the fact that our patients were finding their way through some very difficult spaces.

So, I would tell you not to worry too much about the language or the theory or what you think you're supposed to be doing. Gird yourself sufficiently that you can have a good-enough story going to tolerate the discomfort as you build a better one; one that more clearly fits the facts of yourself and your patients as you go about this arduous but very rewarding business of finding your way through.

I think that Bion has had such a great appeal for me because he was so aware of the subtleties—light and shadow, foreground and background—that help us to find our way through this difficult process. He reminds us to notice the form beneath the content; not to get lost in the particulars that create these false dichotomies between "us" and "them." That type of splitting forces us into untenable positions, such as thinking we should be an expert on someone else's life without really trying to get to know them first, from the inside out.

In the process of trying to understand, something amazing happens. Our nascent understanding feeds that of the other person and we find ourselves embarking on a collaborative journey that is certain to be as terrifying as it is rewarding.

If I leave you with one thought, then, it would be to have faith in yourself, because whatever power you have resides in you. Your greatest gift lies in your ability to see the world from your own perspective, to learn to take the measure of that perspective, and to use that understanding as a means for illuminating the path of the other in whatever role you find yourself, be it teacher, clinician, mother, father, or— most important and overarching all of these—human being.

References

Alvarez, A. (1999), Widening the bridge. *Psychoanal. Dial.*, 9:205–217.

Balint, M. (1953), *Primary Love and Psychoanalytic Technique*. London: Hogarth Press.

Beebe, B. & Lachmann, F. M. (1988), The contributions of mother–infant mutual influence to the origins of self and object representations. *Psychoanal. Psychol.*, 5:305–337.

——— & ——— (1994), Representation and internalization in infancy: Three principles of salience. *Psychoanal. Psychol.*, 11:127–165.

——— & ——— (1998), Co-constructing inner and relational processes: Self and mutual regulation in infant research and adult treatment. *Psychoanal. Psychol.*, 15:480–516.

Bion, W. R. (1961), *Experiences in Groups and Other Papers*. London: Routledge.

——— (1965), *Transformations*. London: Heinemann.

——— (1967a), Notes on memory and desire. *Psychoanal. Forum*, 2:271–280.

——— (1967b), *Second Thoughts: Selected Papers on Psychoanalysis*. Northvale, NJ: Aronson.

——— (1970), *Attention and Interpretation*. London: Heinemann.

——— (1977), *Seven Servants*. New York: Aronson.

——— (1980), *Bion in New York and São Paulo*, ed. F. Bion. Perthshire: Clunie Press.

——— (1991), *A Memoir of the Future*. London: Karnac Books.

Bollas, C. (1987), *The Shadow of the Object: Psychoanalysis of the Unthought Known*. London: Free Association Books.

——— (1992), *Being a Character: Psychoanalysis and Self-Experience*. New York: Hill & Wang.

Brenner, C. (1985), Countertransference as compromise formation. *Psychoanal. Quart.*, 54:155–163.

Brunet, L. & Casoni, D. (2001), A necessary illusion: Projective identification and the containing function. *Canad. J. Psychoanal.*, 9:137–163.

Bucci, W. (1997), Symptoms and symbols: A multiple code theory of somatization. *Psychoanal. Inq.*, 2:151–172.

Charles, M. (1999a), Patterns: Unconscious shapings of self and experience. *J. Melanie Klein and Object Relations*, 17:367–388.

——— (1999b), Sibling mysteries: Enactments of unconscious fears and fantasies. *Psychoanal. Rev.*, 86:927–951.

——— (2000), The intergenerational transmission of unresolved mourning: Personal, familial, and cultural factors. *Samiksa: J. Indian Psychoanal. Soc.*, 54:65–80.

——— (2001a), Assimilating difference: Traumatic effects of prejudice. *Samiksa: J. Indian Psychoanal. Soc.*, 55:15–27.

——— (2001b), Stealing beauty: An exploration of maternal narcissism. *Psychoanal. Rev.*, 88:549–570.

——— (2002a), *Patterns: Building Blocks of Experience*. Hillsdale, NJ: The Analytic Press.

——— (2002b) Bion's grid: A tool for transformation. *J. Amer. Acad. Psychoanal.*, 30:429–445. Also published in French in: *Le Mouvement Psychanalytique*, 4:121–133.

——— (2002c), Through the unknown, remembered gate: Journeys into the labyrinth. *Psychoanal. Rev.*, 89:79–99.

——— (2003), On faith, hope, and possibility. *J. Amer. Acad. Psychoanal.*, 31:687–704.

——— (2004), *Constructing Realities: Transformations Through Myth and Metaphor*. Amsterdam: Rodopi.

Coltart, N. (1992), *Slouching Towards Bethlehem*. New York: Guilford Press.

Ehrenzweig, A. (1967), *The Hidden Order of Art: A Study in the Psychology of Artistic Imagination*. London: Weidenfield & Nicolson.

Fairbairn, W. R. D. (1952), *Psychoanalytic Studies of the Personality*. London: Routledge.

Fogel, A. (1992), Movement and communication in human infancy: The social dynamics of development. *Human Movement Sci.*, 11:387–423.

Freud, S. (1900), The interpretation of dreams. *Standard Edition*, 4 & 5. London: Hogarth Press, 1953.

——— (1910), The future prospects of psycho-analytic therapy. *Standard Edition*, 11:141–151. London: Hogarth Press, 1957.

——— (1914), Remembering, repeating and working-through. *Standard Edition*, 12:147–156. London: Hogarth Press, 1958.

——— (1915), The unconscious. *Standard Edition*, 14:159–215. London: Hogarth Press, 1957.

——— (1921), Group psychology and the analysis of the ego. *Standard Edition*, 18:69–143. London: Hogarth Press, 1955.

——— (1926), Inhibitions, symptoms and anxiety. *Standard Edition*, 20:87–175. London: Hogarth Press, 1959.

Gadamer, H.-G. (1988), *Truth and Method*. New York: Crossroads.

Garfinkle, E. (2003), Towards clarity in psychoanalytic discourse: A consideration defining projective identification as an intrapsychic phantasy. Manuscript submitted for publication.

Gill, M. M. (1979), The analysis of the transference. *J. Amer. Psychoanal. Assn.*, 27:263–288.

Grotstein, J. S. (1981), *Splitting and Projective Identification*. New York: Aronson.

———(2000), *Who is the Dreamer Who Dreams the Dream? A Study of Psychic Presences*. Hillsdale, NJ: The Analytic Press.

———(2002), The light militia of the lower sky: The profounder mission of dreaming and phantasying. Presented at panel Transformations in O: The furthest reaches of the work of Wilfred Bion. J. Grotstein, R. Oelsner & M. Charles. Northern California Society for Psychoanalytic Psychology & the Psychoanalytic Institute of Northern California, San Francisco, September 21.

Guntrip, H. (1989), *Schizoid Phenomena, Object Relations and the Self*. Madison, CT: International Universities Press.

Heimann, P. (1950), On counter-transference. *Internat. J. Psycho-Anal.*, 31:81–84.

Joseph, B. (1997), Projective identification: Some clinical aspects. In: *The Contemporary Kleinians of London*, ed. R. Schafer. Madison, WI: International Universities Press, pp. 100–118.

Kandel, E. R. (1999), Biology and the future of psychoanalysis: A new intellectual framework for psychiatry revisited. *Amer. J. Psychiat.*, 156:505–524.

Klein, M. (1930), The importance of symbol-formation in the development of the ego. In: *Love, Guilt and Reparation and Other Works, 1921–1945*. London: Hogarth Press, 1975, pp. 219–232.

———(1935), A contribution to the psychogenesis of manic-depressive states. In: *Love, Guilt and Reparation and Other Works, 1921–1945*. London: Hogarth Press, 1975, pp. 262–289.

———(1946), Notes on some schizoid mechanisms. In: *Envy and Gratitude and Other Works, 1946–1963*. London: Hogarth Press, 1975, pp. 1–24.

———(1952), The emotional life of the infant. In: *Envy and Gratitude and Other Works, 1946–1963*. London: Hogarth Press, 1975, pp. 61–93.

Knoblauch, S. H. (2000), *The Musical Edge of Therapeutic Dialogue*. Hillsdale, NJ: The Analytic Press.

Krystal, H. (1988), *Integration and Self-Healing: Affect, Trauma, Alexithymia*. Hillsdale, NJ: The Analytic Press.

La Barre, F. (2001), *On Moving and Being Moved: Nonverbal Behavior in Clinical Practice*. Hillsdale, NJ: The Analytic Press.

Lacan, J. (1977), *Ecrits: A Selection*, ed. J.-A. Miller (trans. A. Sheridan). New York: Norton, 1977.

Lachmann, F. M. & Beebe, B. A. (1996), Three principles of salience in the organization of the patient–analyst interaction. *Psychoanal. Psychol.*, 13:1–22.

Langs, R. (1979), *The Therapeutic Environment.* New York: Aronson.

LeDoux, J. E. (1999), Psychoanalytic theory: Clues from the brain. *Neuro-Psychoanalysis*, 1:44–49.

———— (2002), Panel: Trauma, dissociation, and conflict—The space where neuroscience, cognitive science, and psychoanalysis overlap. Presented at "Evolving domains: Psychoanalysis in dialogue with science, culture, and technology," the 22nd annual spring meeting of the American Psychological Association Division of Psychoanalysis (39), New York City, April.

Loewald, H. W. (1951), Ego and reality. *Internat. J. Psycho-Anal.*, 32:10–18.

Levenson, E. A. (1988), The pursuit of the particular: On the psychoanalytic inquiry. *Contemp. Psychoanal*, 24:1–16.

Levin, F. M. (1995), Psychoanalysis and knowledge: Part 1. The problem of representation and alternative approaches to learning. *The Annual of Psychoanalysis*, 23:95–115. Hillsdale, NJ: The Analytic Press.

Mancia, M. (1981), On the beginning of mental life in the foetus. *Internat. J. Psycho-Anal.*, 62:351–357.

Matte-Blanco, I. (1959), Expression in symbolic logic of the characteristics of the system Ucs or the logic of the system Ucs. *Internat. J. Psycho-Anal.*, 40:1–5.

———— (1975), *The Unconscious as Infinite Sets: An Essay in Bi-Logic.* London: Duckworth.

———— (1988), *Thinking, Feeling, and Being: Clinical Reflections on the Fundamental Antinomy of Human Beings and World.* London: Routledge.

McCleary, R. W. (1992), *Conversing With Uncertainty.* Hillsdale, NJ: The Analytic Press.

McDougall, J. (1980), *Plea for a Measure of Abnormality.* New York: International Universities Press.

———— (1985), *Theaters of the Mind: Illusion and Truth on the Psychoanalytic Stage.* New York: Basic Books.

McWilliams, N. (2003), The educative aspects of psychoanalysis. *Psychoanal. Psychol.*, 20:245–260.

Meltzer, D. (1975), Adhesive identification. *Contemp. Psychoanal.*, 11:289–310.

Miall, D. S. & Kuiken, D. (1994), Beyond text theory: Understanding literary response. *Discourse Processes*, 17:337–352.

Ogden, T. H. (1979), On projective identification. *Internat. J. Psycho-Anal.*, 60:357–373.

—— (1985), On potential space. *Internat. J. Psycho-Anal.*, 66:129–141.

—— (1994), The analytic third: Working with intersubjective clinical facts. *Internat. J. Psycho-Anal.*, 75:3–19.

Opatow, B. (1997), Observation and insight in the science of experience. *Amer. Imago*, 54:289–306.

Person, E. S. & Klar, H. (1994), Establishing trauma: The difficulty distinguishing between memories and fantasies. *J. Amer. Psychoanal. Assn.*, 42:1055–1081.

Racker, H. (1972), The meanings and uses of countertransference. *Psychoanal. Quart.*, 41:487–506.

Rayner, E. (1981), Infinite experiences, affects and the characteristics of the unconscious. *Internat. J. Psycho-Anal.*, 62:403–412.

Reich, A. (1951), On counter-transference. *Internat. J. Psycho-Anal.*, 32:25–31.

Saint-Exupéry, A. de (1943), *The Little Prince*, trans. K. Woods. New York: Harcourt, Brace.

Sandler, J. (1976), Countertransference and role-responsiveness. *Internat. Rev. Psycho-Anal.*, 3:43–47.

Sanville, J. (1991), *The Playground of Psychoanalytic Therapy*. Hillsdale, NJ: The Analytic Press.

Segal, H. (1957), Notes on symbol formation. *Internat. J. Psycho-Anal.*, 38:391–397.

—— (1981), *The Work of Hanna Segal: A Kleinian Approach to Clinical Practice*. New York: Aronson.

Shabad, P. (1993), Repetition and incomplete mourning: The intergenerational transmission of traumatic themes. *Psychoanal. Psychol.*, 10:61–75.

Solms, M. (1996), Towards an anatomy of the unconscious. *J. Clinical Psychoanal.*, 5:331–367.

Steiner, J. (1985), Turning a blind eye: The cover up for Oedipus. *Internat. Rev. Psycho-Anal.*, 12:161–172.

Stern, D. N. (1985), *The Interpersonal World of the Infant: A View from Psychoanalysis and Developmental Psychology*. New York: Basic Books.

—— Bruschweiler-Stern, N., Harrison, A. M., Lyons-Ruth, K., Morgan, A. C., Nahum, J. P., Sander, L. & Tronick, E. Z. (1998a), The process of therapeutic change involving implicit knowledge: Some implications of developmental observations for adult psychotherapy. *Infant Mental Health J.*, 19:300–308.

—— Sander, L. W., Nahum, J. P., Harrison, A. M., Lyons-Ruth, K., Morgan, A. C., Bruschweiler-Stern, N. & Tronick, E. Z. (1998b), Non-interpretive mechanisms in psychoanalytic therapy: The 'something more' than interpretation. *Internat. J. Psycho-Anal.*, 79:903–921.

Symington, N. (1983), The analyst's act of freedom as agent of therapeutic change. *Internat. Rev. Psycho-Anal.*, 10:283–291.

Trevarthen, C. (1995), Mother and baby—Seeing artfully eye to eye. In: *The Artful Eye*, ed. R. Gregory, J. Harris, P. Heard & D. Rose. Oxford: Oxford University Press, pp. 157–200.

Tronick, E. (1989), Emotions and emotional communication in infants. *Amer. Psychol.*, 44:112–119.

Tustin, F. (1986), *Autistic Barriers in Neurotic Patients*. New Haven: Yale University Press.

van der Kolk, B. A. (1987), The psychological consequences of overwhelming life experiences. In: *Psychological Trauma*, ed. B. A. van der Kolk. Washington, DC: American Psychiatric Press, pp. 1–30.

Winnicott, D. W. (1965), *The Maturational Processes and the Facilitating Environment*. New York: International Universities Press.

———(1971), *Playing and Reality*. New York: Basic Books.

Index